Praise for All Who Wander

I've been living this book, all my life. It tells the story which I, along with thousands of men, have tried desperately to tell. This book is our platform, a powerful lectern and must read for every young man, every father, every seasoned man . . . every wanderer. This incredible book is a transparent snapshot of one man's life journey, including a period of wandering, which will resonate with nearly all people—especially men. It makes a strong case for the importance of strong fathers and mentors. This story is redemptive. It cheers you on to not give up . . . and rediscover your true purpose.

— ***Mitch Temple***
Co-Founder/ Executive Director,
The Fatherhood CoMission

*A*s one who has wandered a circuitous journey through this life – I can attest to the power of Ralph's testimony. The lessons learned from his experiences are meaningful guideposts for our own sojourn. Ralph provides us with tangible examples of God's omnipresence, how He nudges us along the way. His influence can be found through all of our experiences in life. The reflections in this book remind us of this truth in a deep and poignant way.

— ***John Mulder****, MD*
john.adrian.mulder@gmail.com

D1568334

Every man who has lived for any length of time has faced trials and challenges. It is God's way of bringing us to depend on Him. Ralph Plumb has had one of the most fascinating journeys of anyone I know. It has taken him all over the world, and reading this book reveals that God will always remain faithful to you on your journey. I know this man well. He has become one of my closest friends. You will enjoy reading this and I guarantee it will resonate with you.

— **Don Ankenbrandt**
Creator-Co-author, The 210 Project

I have been a close associate of Dr. Ralph Plumb for about forty years. He is one of the most traveled, well read, highly educated, intelligent, and deeply theological men I have known. He is also a man of prayer. And he learned the invaluable lesson of how to find Peace. Read this book and be inspired!

— **Rufino L. Macagba**, MD, MPH
Chairman, Lorma Medical Center & Colleges

As the medical director of the Christian relief organization where Ralph Plumb served as CEO for ten years, I traveled with him to the far corners of the world. In this inspiring and fascinating book, Ralph shares insights from our travel as well those of his own spiritual journey. He is a man of great integrity. As you will read, he arrived at a place of joy and a spiritual "peace that passes all understanding."

— **Jack A. Henderson**, MD
Former Medical Director of International Aid

$\mathcal{R}$alph and I have been Kingdom co-laborers for decades. With God's grace he has overcome family, social and economic challenges demonstrating the power of human creativity, intellect, spirituality and passion. Being a *philos,* one beloved, he was stretched from a young boy to a man, never to return to his same dimensions. His travels and life journey have made him mature in body, mind and spirit.

— *George M. Bell,* D.Min.
Pastor & Community Advocate

$\mathcal{R}$ead as one-part travel journal ala Paul Theroux, one-part theological treatise ala Charles E. Fuller and one-part personal catharsis /reflection, written as only my dear friend Ralph has proven himself capable of, *All Who Wander* exposes a courageous and gifted "man after God's own heart." As a fellow wanderer, I too have discovered that "love is intended to be both the journey and the destination."

— *Paul B. Thompson*
COO, Plant with Purpose

$\mathcal{I}$t has been my privilege to share some of the memories and deep spiritual lessons Ralph recounts in this book. His ability to connect resources with need is a gift from God that many nations have benefitted from. If you want to know how our Lord provides for desperate people in horrible circumstances read this book and be inspired. It is a testament of God's Spirit living in and working through servants like Ralph!

— *Allison Speer*
Gospel Recording Artist

$\mathcal{R}$alph is authentic, writes with genuine openness, and bares his soul without putting a spin on the difficult moments. In the 40 years I have known and traveled with him, he was always a friend whose earthly pilgrimage paralleled my own. But, as I read his book, I felt like he was a prophet skillfully weaving the temporal with the spiritual, giving me an opportunity to re-examine my own relationships and priorities for the Kingdom. Let Ralph take you to some of the earth's neediest and exotic places. But also, be ready to travel closer to our heavenly home.

*— **Milton A. Amayun,** MD, MPH*
Global Health Advisor

$\mathcal{R}$alph uniquely weaves his real-life experiences and global travel to bring fresh insights on life, eternity and other important topics. Each chapter will challenge you to live with an eternal perspective, while living life to the fullest. His writing will encourage you to live beyond the complacent ... something often missing in our society today.

*— **Gary Martin,** Sr Pastor*
The Bridge Church

$\mathcal{R}$alph draws deeply from the well of his own experience of ministry, travel and life challenges in this engaging memoir. Readers will enjoy the stories from his years of travel, knit together with lessons learned and meditations on Scripture, the nature of God and his universe.

*— **Robert E. Logan,** PhD*
Logan Leadership

ALL WHO
WANDER

Jef,   3-23-23

Life is an intersting journey . . .

We experience both joy and pain, success and failure. We have both times of wonder and wandering. God brings us through it all if we seek Him and trust completely in His sovereignty and then . . .

we become one of His wounded healers.

Abundant blessings,

[signature]

Joshua 1:9

ALL WHO
WANDER

*Rediscover God's Purpose
on Your Journey*

RALPH EDWARD PLUMB

ILLUMIFY
MEDIA.COM
WE BRING YOUR BOOK TO LIFE!

ALL WHO
WANDER

Published by
Illumify Media Global
www.IllumifyMedia.com
"We bring your book to life!"

Library of Congress Control Number: 2020924800

Paperback ISBN: 978-1-949021-64-6
eBook ISBN: 978-1-949021-65-3

Typeset by Art Innovations (http://artinnovations.in/)
Cover design by Debbie Lewis

Printed in the United States of America

Dedication

I honor you, Lord. Thank you, for your redeeming grace and mercy. Never once did you leave me.

And I am eternally indebted to those faithful saints whom I have met in every corner of the world, who model what it means to trustfully surrender to your sovereignty in *all* circumstances.

Contents

Foreword

*W*hat you are about to read is an amazing global journey to some of the most exotic and inaccessible places on earth. This is also a story about a man's spiritual journey to discover meaning and embrace his purpose—and then to rediscover it after losing his way.

As a Christian psychologist, I have been helping good men find their way along the unpredictable path of life for more than three decades. Previous generations had role models and generally accepted definitions of masculinity that made it a lot clearer to know who they were as a man, and where they were going. That has all changed. Our role as men and the very foundations of the traditional family are under attack as never before. Sometimes we find ourselves at a place where we just don't know. It's no wonder many of us find ourselves lost, at some point. I am grateful for men like Ralph Plumb who, in this book, tells us his story of faithfully following God, encountering some hard-hitting challenges, wandering through a period of uncertainty, then finding his way back. From my professional experience, I know there a lot of men who will relate.

Men were not raised to be vulnerable and honest about their emotions, especially with other men. We were raised to be competitors, successful, strong, and silent. These are all good things (except for too much silence, at times). But these qualities are not enough for us be complete men. Men today need to admit when we are lost, ask for help, and open up about how we feel. Healthy masculinity requires vulnerability and honesty. It takes a lot of courage for a man to open up. Men are vilified in sitcoms, assumed to be sexist until proven innocent, and accused of the lust for dominance because of their testosterone. To open up with the kind of vulnerability that Ralph displays here is rare. I commended him highly for this. If you are inclined, write him yourself and explain your journey. Doing this can be part of your healing process.

Ralph's story is sobering, because bad things can and do happen to good men too. We were led to believe if we accept Christ, marry a decent Christian woman, and raise our kids to follow Jesus everything is supposed to end alright. But if you take a closer look at men and women in the Bible you will see that life rarely turns out that way. Even God-honoring people have marriages that don't work out, kids who don't turn out as planned, and who sometimes give up on God for a season. Our Lord has given us the ability to choose our path in life. That means things don't always go in the direction we hoped they would. But this book also affirms that we have a loving and redemptive Father who is ready to take us back when we reach out to him.

So, what happens to a man when he wanders off the path? At first, most men don't even know they are wandering. In fact, they think they are making good progress. If you ask, they will say, "Well, look how much further along I am than that guy over there!" When a man finally realizes that he has been wandering around trying to find the right direction for his life, he comes face-to-face with a powerful emotion, the very emotion that caused him to lose his direction in the first place: shame.

Why do men wander? I think Ralph describes it well. We don't wander off the path because we are looking for something; it's because we are trying to hide something we can't quite define and wish we didn't have. At the deepest level, good men wander because we have been painfully injured by life and can't admit it, which results in shame. We have been told our whole lives to do something (chapter

3, "Doing versus Being"), to know what we are doing (chapter 4, "Wisdom or Knowledge"), and since we are free to make our own choices in life—we'd better get it right (chapter 7, "Freedom Is Not Free"). But no matter how good you are, no one can ever get it right enough to avoid feeling like a failure at something. What we most often fail at is our relationships with God and the people closest to us.

There is a difference between guilt and shame. Guilt is the painful feeling of *doing* something wrong; shame is the painful feeling of *being* something wrong. It's much worse. You can repent of the things you have done wrong, and ask for forgiveness (chapter 13, "Forgiveness and Healing"). As hard as it is for a man to confess his guilt, that's really important to do. But what's the solution for *being* something wrong? This is so hard to figure out that many men try to stuff this feeling of shame deep inside, act like they know what they are doing, and wander off into the sunset so everyone will think they are on a really important mission.

How does a man overcome this painful feeling of shame that is at the root of his wandering? Thankfully, there is an answer: grace (chapter 12, "Grace and Mercy"). But grace is not an idea, nor a concept that can be conquered intellectually. It is an experience of unmerited acceptance that overcomes the lie that a man is unworthy of love. Men wander and miss the mark because we have a hidden painful feeling of unworthiness that we try to escape until it is addressed. Once we come face-to-face with this painful feeling of shame, we have a choice: we can continue to try to cover it over with great wanderings, accomplishments, and other self-medications, or we can do the very thing that shame tells us not to do—vulnerably surrender to God.

Then, paradoxically, instead of feeling more shame for exposing ourselves, we actually find that this is the only true source of healing for our pain. Grace heals shame. That's just how God made the world. When a man learns this truth, he doesn't need to wander anymore. He has found his healing home, right there in front of him where it was the entire time.

Dr. Mark W. Baker
Author, *Overcoming Shame: Let Go of Others'*
Expectations and Embrace God's Acceptance;
and, *Jesus: The Greatest Therapist Who Ever Lived*

Preface

One of the decorative souvenirs hanging on my wall is a simple wooden plaque that reads, "All who wander are not lost." This seems logical. However, I am inclined to believe, from my own experience and reading, that this statement would have broader application and greater truth if it read, "All who wander *may* not be lost, but many are . . . and searching."

Acclaimed by the *Daily Telegraph* as a literary masterpiece, the 933-page book *Shantaram* by Gregory David Roberts is a riveting read. His back-cover summary teases, "An armed robber and heroin addict, escaped from an Australian prison to India, where he lived in a Bombay slum. There, he established a free health clinic and also joined the mafia." I've never met or talked with the author, and have no idea if he ever came to faith in Jesus Christ, though the last line of his book reads, "God help us. God forgive us. We live on."[1] Thankfully, my life did not follow a similar path, but had its own unique challenges. My prayer is that you who *may* be still wandering will find your way.

I have always been in a *big* hurry, for what reasons I am still only partially aware. Reflecting more intensely on my patterns of behavior over the years has been enlightening. From a young age I was perpetually impatient with anyone who did not think, talk, or function at my warp speed of living. The word "slow" is still anathema to me. To this day I seldom read an entire email, text, or chat message—and *for sure*, not all the attachments. On phone calls or in-person conversations I am usually finished listening before the person is finished talking. A normal night's sleep is about five hours, with me awakening usually between 3 and 4 a.m., nearly always without an alarm. My mind is always in high gear. God blessed me with relentless energy. But how we deploy our assets and use our talents can sometimes turn a strength into a liability.

An epiphany occurred in my teen years during a church youth group activity. Each picked a name out of a hat and impersonated that person's behavior, while the rest of us had to guess who it was. Eventually someone picked my name, then acted out a hyperactive person flailing his arms and mouthing some rapid-fire gibberish. Without thinking I said, "Who *is* that?" And everyone shouted in unison, pointing to me, "It's *you!*" "Huh? Me?" How did I not recognize it? Perhaps the better question is, why? Most of us can figure out the who, what, when, where, and how of a situation. But our eternal quest for *why* seldom seems clear. What created this need for constant motion? Where was I headed—and why? What type of work would require this level of energy?

My perspective, now looking back, is that while I accomplished much in my life, taking time to build relationships and to enjoy simple, restful discoveries were often missed along the way. I asked Jesus into my heart and accepted him as Savior at age nineteen. Almost immediately, I brought him along *with me* rather than first seeking his guidance, though I did pray for it. Praying but not listening. It took decades for me to fully understand the deep value of quiet, spiritual reflection. God *does* speak to us . . . but in a still, small voice. And only when we wait upon his Holy Spirit.

One of my lifelong passions is travel. I recall looking out the bedroom window of my childhood Connecticut home, during all four seasons, and imagining what was *out there.* An early love of reading kept me immersed in stories about people and places I would eventually meet and experience. I even offered up some nascent prayers to the God I did not yet fully know, asking that he allow me to see the world. Having now worked in or traveled in about one hundred countries, I can accept the moniker of world traveler. I have been "on the road" and in the air for over two million miles. Where does "wandering" play a role in this journey—yours and mine?

One definition of wandering suggests a person who will "go from place to place aimlessly." This hardly reflects my life. I was always driven and on a mission. Yet, when we consider our spiritual search for meaning, there *is* some aimless uncertainty . . . some wandering. The eighteenth-century hymn by Robert Robinson so aptly describes the spiritual wandering of our human condition: "Jesus sought me when a stranger, wandering from the fold of God. . . . Bind my wandering heart to Thee. Prone to wander, Lord I feel it, prone to leave the God I love; here's my heart, O take and seal it, seal it for Thy courts above."

The wandering I reflect on in this book is the uncertain path of rediscovering the purpose of my life journey after a series of crucible events. Some were out of my control. Others were of my own doing. We each have an amazing opportunity to live in an intimate relationship with our Creator. No two roads of discovery are exactly the same. Because this is true, I simply wish to share some of what I learned along the way, both by human happenstance and divine intent. Certain truths I discovered will apply to your journey and others will not. One thing I am certain of: this journey, our road of wandering if you will, has both a starting point and a destination. As one song lyric suggests, we may never pass this way again. Geographically that could be true. Sometimes we will visit a place only once. But in terms of time and conscious experience we will *never* pass the same way again.

It is nothing short of amazing to realize that God sees the end from the beginning. If you believe there *is* absolute truth, it is up to *you* to search for it until you find it. One of my most treasured discoveries— only too recently—is that peace and happiness come from *total* trustful surrender to our loving Father, "who is, and who was, and who is to come" (Rev. 1:8). I'd like to share how I got here, over the past roughly forty years.

Our time of wandering may not happen in a single linear plane. It often doesn't work that way. We know from experience, and also from Ecclesiastes, that there is a time and season for everything under heaven: infancy, youth, education, job, marriage, kids, achievement, satisfaction, legacy, grandkids, golden years, and sunset. Unfortunately, there are quite a few more dynamics which come crashing into these life stages at various points, destroying the Norman Rockwell-esque dreams we might like to see fulfilled: failure, disappointment, illness, death, bone-weariness, doubt, fear, tragedy, anger, shame, aimlessness, periods of inertia. A lexicon of maladies and stumbling blocks get in our way.

So, we're going along doing just fine, thank you . . . then "it" happens. "It" is not the same for each of us. "It" may be betrayal, divorce, cancer, death of a loved one, financial ruin, or the feeling that we have lost our inner compass. But whatever "it" is will most certainly strike at our core in a profound way. We become disoriented, find ourselves in a wilderness of self-doubt, on a darkened path, suddenly not sure if we're on the right path, or if we should have taken the road less traveled. We wonder if God has abandoned us because we were stupid enough to get involved in, or involved with, [fill in the blank]. Each one sneaks up and bites us.

Scripture tells us, "We all, like sheep, have gone astray, each of us has turned to our own way" (Isa. 53:6). This passage is well understood by a pastoral society of centuries past, familiar with the behavior of sheep. Today I suspect the writer might say: *everyone screws up sometime.* Yet God is there to welcome us back when we humbly and earnestly seek him!

For years I boarded an untold number of international flights. On these mostly missions of mercy, I saw unimaginable suffering in places ravaged by war, famine, natural disasters, and man-made crises. So many people crying out for God's light in a dark place. I would like to share some real stories of memorable people and places as seen through my eyes, captured in about fifty-three travel journals. I'd also like to share a few lessons I learned, *the hard way*, about struggling through the unplanned for "it"s that happened at a few stages of my life. In God's providence, these had the greatest impact for good and necessary change.

What makes us truly wise? For sure it includes the passing of time, the honest embrace of failure then getting up again, the necessity that we forgive, and allowing ourselves to truly grieve unavoidable sorrow. As I traveled around the globe, busy and active, at times searching, I *finally* discovered some of God's deepest truths.

My final thought, valued reader and fellow wanderer, is that I hope to communicate as a fountain, not a firehose. This book is about the path *I* took and what God taught *me*. Take what is of value to you and leave the rest to someone else. To the wandering soul who has yet to encounter God in a personal way for the first time, please keep asking and seeking. But to the believer, the Christ-follower, who has somehow lost your way, had your faith battered, or had your confidence undermined, I can tell you from experience: there is newness of life beyond spiritual inertia, apathy, or even a temporary prodigal falling away. God's light and love, his forgiveness and mercy, are always and readily available to us!

Introduction

*I*t's hard to steer a parked car. Obviously, the car needs to be operable and it needs to be in gear. Once that occurs, and assuming the car is not stuck in a ditch somewhere, it will start to move on some type of surface, leaving its starting point toward some destination. Along the way, both car and driver will pass a kaleidoscope of color and a cacophony of sound. An important question to ask is: Who is steering the car? It's the driver, of course. But *who* is *steering the driver*?

With a bit of imagination, this metaphor also describes our life. We exist. We need to be able to function. There is much to see and experience on the way. Something or some One is directing us. And we *are* moving toward some destination, whether we realize it or not. The rock group the Eagles adds another element to this story from their classic song "Hotel California": "Some dance to remember. Some dance to forget." What is it about *your* life journey that you would prefer to forget? And where are you headed?

I have been on the road most of my life, literally, figuratively . . . and spiritually. And in all three categories it has been "a long and winding road." I was born to an unwed mother and adopted by a loving, simple man at age five. His name was Chauncey, and I called him Dad. I never knew or met my natural father. Dad's high school education was sufficient to secure a manufacturing job in a dirty powdered metal company where he labored for years. He came home every day looking like he had finished a shift in a coal mine. Toward the end of his "career" he graduated to quality-control parts inspector, a time clock-punching hourly job where he stared at a conveyor belt for imperfections in the tens of thousands of fabricated metal pieces per day that plodded past his heavily spectacled eyes. The tedium and repetition would have crushed my soul. But he faithfully brought home his pay to care for his contentious wife and adopted son. I had no siblings.

Our dwelling was 640 square feet, with one bedroom. My parents gave me the bedroom. They slept on an uncomfortable fold-out couch with a cheap four-inch mattress on squeaky springs in the "living room." The rest of the décor included one gaudy armchair, a TV, and an upright piano that collected dust since no one could play it. The only other room in the house, besides a postage-stamp-sized bathroom, was the kitchen. It was the indisputable domain of my natural mother Louise, who talked endlessly, stomping heavily back and forth across the faded linoleum flooring on the few square feet of movable space. Clutter was everywhere. Occasionally she would tip over the stacked-to-the-ceiling, used but washed Styrofoam trays and plastic containers, vestiges of her Depression-era pack-rat habits. These containers came from endless quantities of inexpensive processed foods that we purchased at a discount food outlet. I was a chubby kid then, because nutritional balance did not exist.

Unlike the rest of the house, I kept my room neat and orderly, too embarrassed to invite any friends over. I spent most of my at-home time playing outside or in my room with the door shut reading and dreaming of traveling. Watching television or movies, or digital gaming, to this day, seems like a complete waste of time. I would stare out my window for hours and *imagine*. That Eagles song, now playing in my head, makes perfect sense.

As an only child, and out of emotional necessity, I learned to be self-sufficient. I was perfectly comfortable initiating and pursuing many things—sports, academics, theatre, small income-generating ventures. I would hike alone in the beautiful summer greenery and fall colors of our region. With the exception of winter, I would drag used scraps of wood to my yard from construction sites and build forts. Or I would ride my bike across town to play with friends who were not invited to my house. For years, I accompanied Mom to pick up Dad from his work shift, because we only had one old car to take us all where we needed to go. I watched streams of men running to their cars after the factory horn blasted, leaving the drudgery of their daily existence. I realized early on that I had better get my butt in gear and find a way to make a living that best utilized the unique gifting God had given me.

In high school I pushed myself—student government, and three-sport athlete. I only excelled in soccer. In my senior year I was the co-captain of our regional champion soccer team and high-goal scorer as center striker. I was selected to play Curly, the male lead in Rogers and Hammerstein's *Oklahoma*. Our local high school had developed a reputation for vaunted senior class productions put on with Broadway-quality sets, costumes, and performances. I completed my Eagle Scout rank at seventeen. Eventually, I pursued not one but four degrees, which I paid for myself.

A friend and pastor in Spring Lake, Michigan, also named Ralph, told me years later that eagles do not fly in flocks. He observed my relentless drive and determination with the tendency to lead, not follow. I have heard the same sentiment expressed in two other ways. One Iditarod Trail sled-dog musher, who raced from Anchorage to Nome, was overheard saying, "Unless you're the lead dog, the scenery never changes." But the most memorable window into who I was, who God made me to be, was shaped by our tough but effective Gunny (Gunnery Sergeant) at the Naval Education and Training Center in Newport, Rhode Island who barked at us while our officers-in-training class ran P.T. to always push to be "top dog." I graduated as a newly minted Lieutenant Junior Grade in the Chaplain Corps with a "conquer the world" attitude about the future. Navy chaplains also proudly serve the Marines and these were most of my duty stations over the eight years that I served.[1]

After the unknown "father" void in my psycho social development during my pre-adoption years, and after enough education to make me think I actually *knew* what I was doing, I started on the road I had prepared for. My goal was to work in an international context and the first job I pursued was with a nonprofit. After just two years, I reached a potentially life-changing fork in the road. From California I was flown to south Florida and offered a corporate job with American Express, at a significantly higher starting salary. Nearly simultaneously, I was selected for an international posting in Taipei, Taiwan, to coordinate programs serving refugees and displaced persons throughout southeast Asia. After praying about it, I concluded that I would take the road of service. To this day I'm glad I made that decision. Making money has never been a primary motivation for me. In God's providence, the path I chose turned out to be the adventure of a lifetime. For nearly twenty years I kept a tattered fortune cookie saying in my wallet which read, "Life to you is a bold and dashing adventure." It most certainly has been. Let me tell you about some of those adventures and some special people I met on my journey.

These travel experiences in twenty-seven countries include historical and cultural items of interest, supplemented with observations from my journals. But this is equally a spiritual memoir, with both achievement and failure, towering faith and withering commitment, which God in his abundant mercy used to shape me into the man he created me to be.

Chapter One

ON THE ROAD

There was nowhere to go but everywhere, so just keep on rolling under the stars. **— Jack Kerouac**

*M*y journey to "the roof of the world"—Lhasa, Tibet—with my dear friend John Mulder, MD, and two other associates was a kick. John is a remarkable man. He began as a family practice physician, delivering more than three thousand babies during the first half of his career. He then sensitively served older adults facing difficult end-of-life decisions and those needing palliative care or hospice. He is also a multi-CD songwriter and performer.

Lhasa is the holy city of Tibetan Buddhism, and the political, economic, and cultural center of the so-called Tibet Autonomous Region, which the Han Chinese from Beijing now control with an iron fist. The Potala Palace—a UNESCO World Heritage Site, and winter palace of each Dalai Lama from 1649–1959—was the first place we wanted to visit. The current Dalai Lama, of course, was exiled (escaped) to India in 1959 when the communists arrived by force and decided he was *persona non grata*. This magnificent thirteen-story structure with one thousand rooms, chock full of tapestries and artifacts, towers over the city. It is the burial place of all thirteen Dalai Lamas; burial sites #1–4 were desecrated (destroyed) during the Cultural Revolution, and sites #5–13 are now a source of tourist revenue for the Chinese.

Potala Palace

We had one of two options to prepare ourselves for the 11,995-foot elevation—acetazolamide, which reduces the more acute symptoms of altitude sickness with some side effects; or downing gallons of water while traveling to minimize the pounding headaches. We opted for the latter, which *did* help our high-altitude discomfort. We laughed when we realized this gave new meaning to the phrase, "Drink like a fish." Choosing this option required roadside pit stops to take a pee about every hour on the hour. What a sight we made: every few kilometers, on Tibet's potholed dusty roads, five guys—including the driver, of course—would be lined up doing his business. Fortunately, no transit buses passed us in this remote area. While traveling we continued to admire the staggeringly beautiful snow-covered peaks in the distance— some sixty-plus of them, miles beyond Lhasa, which ranged in elevation from 14,000 to more than 26,000 feet. We passed deep, clear lakes that reflected like mirrors. And the blinding, azure, cloudless sky required the highest number SPF sunblock and wrap-around sunglasses.

With tickets in hand for the tour of the Potala the following day, John returned. "Hey Ralph, I found a great place for dinner. They serve world-famous yak burgers."

"No kidding," I replied, "I wonder if yak burgers taste anything like the meat we ate at the Carnivore Restaurant outside Nairobi?"

"The place is called Snow Land Restaurant and they even have apple pie a la mode," John continued for emphasis. With no objections from the others, we walked the relatively short distance, grabbed a table in this busy gathering place of people from East and West, and enjoyed an upbeat and pleasant evening. It wasn't hard to notice the single dour and fidgety man in grey clothes at an adjacent table, smoking like a chimney. We knew he was our Chinese government *minder,* assigned to watch us and report any deviation from the approved playbook.

The next morning before our midday tour John took off for a couple of hours then came back with enough purchased souvenirs to sink the Bismarck.

"Jeez-o-peet, John. What did you buy?"

"Well, I have a lot of people to shop for," he reasoned. He showed us his newly acquired treasures. After seeing his range of trinkets, we all agreed that we too would visit the Jokhar Bazaar after our Potala tour. My purchases, as always, were much smaller, lighter, and fewer. But the primary memory etched in my mind from that shopping excursion was seeing four Chinese military pull a hapless, non-struggling man out of his souvenir shop and beat the crap out of him, kicking him in places I wouldn't want to experience. Then they dragged him into a waiting van, shuttering his shop, and posted a sentry outside. When the commotion was over, I asked a neighboring vendor who could speak English what happened. "Why did the authorities come for that man and close his shop?"

He replied, "He was caught selling Dalai Lama souvenirs. He isn't the only one. We have to be much more careful these days. This is illegal in Tibet now." I let that sink in for a bit. The political oppression of Tibetans remains to this day.

As we returned to our Lhasa Hotel, we passed the Jokhang Temple where many pilgrims from remote villages walked clockwise around the facility turning their prayer wheels.

Jokhang Temple

Our trip here wasn't for pleasure, however. Our medical team met with both Tibetan health practitioners and expatriate medical staff to discuss ways to mitigate the chronic tuberculosis in the population and address the physical and emotional aftermath of the forced abortions imposed on the village women who had to comply with the then-new Chinese *one-child policy*.[1] The people in the villages were poor, but gracious and friendly.

Tibetan family   *Tibetan girl*

We took a bone-jarring eight-hour journey to Shigatse passing glaciers, live wandering yaks that weren't ground up into burgers, and meandering mountain dwellers with deep, bronze, sunbaked faces. As we continued, we occasionally passed clusters of prayer flags flapping in the stiff breeze. My final journal entry was this: *I leave Tibet with a sense of mission accomplished. We've set up our remote, primary health support program for the rural health workers. But I leave with a sense of dis-ease for the future of these beautiful people. Potala, says it all. It is nearly empty in spirit, like a museum devoid of its greatest treasure.*

In those days I traveled extensively. Only a few weeks later I was on a plane again, this time to Yunnan Province in southern China which borders Vietnam, Laos, and Burma. For one full decade, I traveled with Chen Min Yen (George), a Christian evangelist and pastor. My role was to coordinate resources to the ethnic minority communities he served, to build or supply clinics, churches, and schools through his ministry. When Mao took over and instituted his series of repressive pogroms— The Great Leap Forward, the Cultural Revolution, and the Red Guard period—George represented the triple sin of being educated, being Christian, and being the son of an industrialist, *a capitalist pig.*

Called to serve the Lord at age eighteen, Chen responded, leaving his home and family in his native Shanghai. Sailing up the Yangtze River into the Changjiang River Valley, he began full-time ministry, bringing the gospel to the many ethnic minorities populating the rural and mountain villages. His efforts quickly attracted the attention of communist officials. Just two years after beginning his ministry, Chen was arrested and imprisoned, for the heinous crime of building a church. Released a few months later, he returned to his work and was arrested again, this time for publishing hymnbooks for the churches. Released again, he planted a new church, which quickly grew to three hundred. This final disobedience proved to be his undoing—or as I see it, God's design for his transformation into a true saint. This time his arrest offered no early release.

By now China's communist government was steadfastly attempting to eradicate all religions in its 9.59 million square kilometers of control by regularly raiding religious sites and banning religious materials. They aggressively persecuted, imprisoned, and sometimes murdered Muslim, Buddhist, Taoist, Christian, and other religious leaders throughout the country.

Pastor George Chen

If you think present-day China is any different, or better, under current strongman Xi Jinping, it is *not*! In fact, China's oppression is more insidious, widespread, and brutal under the present-day Chinese Communist Party (CCP). The Uighurs in Xinjiang are being "re-educated" en masse. Hong Kong's freedom under the "one country two systems" agreement until 2047 is now out the window. Mongolia's language and culture are being removed from their educational system. The ultimate goal of Chairman Xi and the CCP is the subjugation of Taiwan and its forced reintegration into the motherland. This is a ticking time bomb that, I predict, *will* occur in the relatively near future. In my years of travel in China I have seen police kick into the air small boards with neatly stacked vegetables resting on two flat stones, attended by a row of squatting saleswomen, because they were a few inches further into the roadway than acceptable. In our rented van circumventing Tiananmen Square, a heavily armed law enforcement person kicked in the van's accordion door entrance, shouting at the driver to grill him on our origins. My mind drifts back now to what I realized was *true* police brutality.

"We knew if we didn't join the government-endorsed Three-Self Church[2] we could be arrested," Chen said. "I had been thrice warned. But by then, I had a hard-boiled heart. I could not stop my ears and refuse to hear the Word of God." The price of such faith came high. Convicted on charges of subversion, Chen was sentenced to eighteen years of hard labor. Along with sixty thousand other undeserving souls, they were worked to exhaustion in a reeducation camp. Pastor George posed a triple threat to the mighty atheist rulers of Maoist China. His duty in the camp was to work in the cesspool, harvesting human waste. They used this as fertilizer for the collective farm which inadequately fed these unfortunate souls. Wading into the two-meter deep trench *each* morning seven days a week, he was given only a shovel to remove successive layers of human waste.

George and I traveled together to encourage the hard-working Lisu mountain people, living at elevations of ten thousand feet or higher. The path to their village was seldom wider than eighteen inches.

Approaching Lisu Village

Entire Lisu Village

When we stopped for a rest break, George completed his stunning testimony: "All the day I had to breath the most-foul air, the most maddening stench." He continued with a steely eyed look on his face, "The cesspool was the only place I had any solitude because the cadres would remove themselves because of the smell. Everyone else being reeducated were subject to constant surveillance, blaring music, and propaganda messages. But I had many, many hours to myself when I could sing hymns, pray, and recite Scripture at the top of my voice. At those times, I felt the Lord's presence with me, and I heard the Lord say I was His own. He never left me. He never forsook me. At that moment, the cesspool became my private garden."

You *too* are on the road, on your own journey. Has it gone the way you planned? Are you still certain of the path you are on? Whichever phase of life you find yourself will determine the things which matter most. For those of us in the third trimester of our time on earth there is an increased sensitivity to our mortality, an awareness of what we still want to accomplish, and a realization that relationships mean the most, some which still need repair. For many, we embrace a deep desire to live in closer communion with the One who created us. We may not be traveling on physical roads or planes as much now, but our wandering heart still seeks its divinely inbred anchorage. Each one of us *is* on a uniquely individual road to discover meaning and purpose. We *will* encounter the living Christ if we seek to do so. Regardless of our human condition, God's love desires us. He *is* waiting for us.

Consider the following three encounters with Christ in the Bible. Does this reflect different places in your faith journey? While Saul "was still breathing out murderous threats against the Lord's disciples" on one of his journey's to Syria he was specifically looking for any "who belonged to The Way" (Acts 9:1–2). Whether man or woman, his goal was to take them as prisoners to Jerusalem. "As he neared Damascus on his journey, suddenly a light from heaven flashed around him. He fell to the ground and heard a voice say to him, 'Saul, Saul why do you persecute me?' 'Who are you, Lord?' Saul asked. 'I am Jesus whom you are persecuting'" (Acts 9:3–5).

Then consider the man on the road to Jericho who was attacked, stripped naked, pistol-whipped, and robbed. The good people of Israel walked past him. But a person of a different faith and culture spent time and money to extend the mercy of Jesus which he taught his disciples; a lesson for each of us. "Go and do likewise" (Luke 10:37).

Then we read about the two new disciples walking to Emmaus discussing the crucifixion of their Messiah and what it would mean for their future. They did not initially recognize Jesus as he appeared and walked with them. When he asked what they were discussing, Cleopas said, "we *had* hoped that he was the one who was going to redeem Israel" (Luke 24:21, emphasis added). They likely walked and talked for hours more until the sun began to set and they arrived at their intended village. The two disciples asked Jesus to stay with them. It was during the evening meal when Jesus took the bread, broke it, prayed, and gave it to them that their eyes were opened. When they returned to Jerusalem, they sought out the eleven disciples and excitedly told them, "It is true! The Lord has risen" (Luke 24:34). He *has* risen indeed!

Which story best fits your experience? Do you forcefully oppose others who are different than you? Are you a decent and giving person, doing your best to help when you see someone in need? Do you follow Christ, but question or lose sight of his promises? At various points in my life, I have been Saul, the Samaritan, and Cleopas.

It has taken me too many decades to *begin* to grasp, to understand even an infinitesimal amount of truth, about our heavenly Father's majesty and eternal love for me—for all of us! I've lived most of my life trying to run it myself, fingers gripping on the steering wheel. I *did* try, but inconsistently, to trust him in all things. Finally, I realized that he is *so* much better at directing my life than I am. Over the years, how often did I find myself wandering in stubborn independence or foolish disobedience with the wrong focus and priorities? "All men seek for Me, but all men do not know what they want. They are seeking because they are dissatisfied, without realizing that I am the object of their quest."[3] Even today, when in doubt, God *still* assures me, still assures *you*, that he loves us, that he is still with us. And as we travel on our unique road of life, he eternally beckons us to share this love with others.

Chapter 2

TIME AND ETERNITY

The day which we fear as our last is but the birthday of eternity. — **Lucius A. Seneca**

*U*ntil Starbucks stopped selling papers, I would read all six published weekly editions of *The Wall Street Journal* at my favorite local hangout, while drinking my tall iced Americano with an extra shot, light ice. I now receive the *WSJ* on home delivery—and ironically, travel fewer times to my local Starbucks, spending less money on coffee. The headline one particular day was, "Scientists Release First Image of a Black Hole."[1] It was accompanied by a color photo of a somewhat blurry circular donut shaped object with gradient hues of bright yellow, orange, and red, with black in the donut hole center and a black background surrounding the central focal point of the photo. The article went on to say, "The intensely dense hole, 6.5 billion times as massive as the sun, is located at the center of a massive galaxy 55 million light years from Earth. Scientists revealed the first image of a black hole, providing a peek at an object once thought to be unseeable and confirming some of Albert Einstein's longstanding theories about general relativity."

I had forgotten much of my limited science training, and for sure didn't recall what the distance of a light year is, so I did a web search for it. The result: 5.879×10^{12}, or to round off, nearly six trillion miles.

This gigantic black hole, located in Galaxy M87, was captured through the powerful Event Horizon Telescope, a planet-scale array of eight ground-based radio telescopes, requiring international cooperation. You won't be able to do the calculation on your smart phone because there is not enough digit space—58 million times 6 trillion! I can't get my brain wrapped around a number that size let alone the actual distance it represents. And this is just in *one* galaxy far, far away. What then does this say about the universe?

"The heavens declare the glory of God; the skies proclaim the work of his hands" (Ps. 19:1). When I look up on a clear night sky, I can literally feel the presence of our Creator. It elicits praise and thanks from my innermost being. Some of us live in urban areas where the astronomical number of twinkling stars in the night sky are not so vibrant. Even then, you may have a similar reaction. We not only "see" with our eyes, but also with our spirit. However, not everyone perceives in the same manner or with the same outcome.

Let me tell you a portion of a larger story about two men you likely have familiarity with. They even have the same first name, though spelled differently.

Stephen Hawking, the Cambridge physicist and cosmologist (a person who studies the cosmos) is considered one of the most intelligent persons in the modern era. One of his books, *A Brief History of Time*, covers such topics as space and time, elementary particles and forces of nature, time travel, worm holes and black holes, the unification of physics, and more. Stephen achieved much beyond his physical limitations caused by amyotrophic lateral sclerosis (ALS, also called Lou Gehrig's disease). He was wheelchair-bound and could only communicate through a small sensor activated by a muscle in his cheek. Stephen died in 2018 a resolute agnostic. He believed "Heaven is a myth, a fairy tale for people afraid of the dark." Among his last words were these, "No one created our universe, and no one directs our fate.

This leads me to a profound realization: There is *probably* no heaven, and no afterlife. We have this one life to appreciate the grand design of the universe, and for that I am extremely grateful."[2] Psalm 14:1 shares a different perspective, "The fool says in his heart there is no God."

Steven Jobs, an American business magnate, industrial designer, and inventor, will always be remembered for co-founding Apple. Except for those who knew him well, he is less recognized for being chair and majority shareholder of Pixar, significant board member and influencer of the Walt Disney Company, founder and CEO of NeXT, and more. He was born to two University of Wisconsin graduate students who gave him up for adoption. Jobs was extremely smart, but spiritually directionless. He was not considered an empathetic person, but instead was abrasive and extremely driven. His life was cut short at age fifty-six after succumbing to pancreatic adenocarcinoma (cancer) in 2011. Among his last words were these: "I reached the pinnacle of success in the business world. In others' eyes, my life is an epitome of success. However, aside from my work, I have little joy. . . . At this moment, lying in a sick bed and recalling my whole life, I realize that all the recognition of wealth that I took so much pride in, have paled and become meaningless in the face of impending death. . . . Oh wow. Oh wow. Oh wow!"[3] What could his *very last* six recorded words suggest? What did he see? Where was he going?

What is the relationship between space and time? I don't know about you, but I seldom ponder this. Most of us try not to think much about time, *especially* our mortality. What we do know is that when we were kids our summers between school seemed like an eternity. Now, without question, the older we get the faster time passes, or so it seems. "We are but a moment's sunlight fading in the grass."[4] A friend remarked, "Don't complain about growing old. Many, many people do not have that privilege." In today's world we are engaged in using renewable resources—energy, such as solar, wind, hydro, and geothermal; as well as biodegradables, such as straws, shopping bags, cups, and plates. But when you think about it, *time* is our most precious *non*renewable resource. Or *is* it nonrenewable? When our time is gone, we are gone. Or are we?

Thankfully, we will *not* always live within the confines of time. Let's consider another source of truth: "He has made everything beautiful in its time. He has also set eternity in the human heart; yet no one can fathom what God has done from beginning to end" (Eccl. 3:11). "Why you do not even know what will happen tomorrow. What is your life? You are a mist that appears for a while and then vanishes" (Jas. 4:14). This is not the whole story, though, for the person who knows and trusts in God! "Therefore, we do not lose heart. Though outwardly we are wasting away, yet inwardly we are being renewed day by day. For our light and momentary troubles are achieving for us an eternal glory that far outweighs them all. So, we fix our eyes not on what is seen, but on what is unseen, since what is seen is temporary, but what is unseen is eternal" (2 Cor. 4:16–18).

Nearly every ancient culture looked toward the heavens, attempted to discern the origins of life, and then applied their limited understanding to its meaning. Their divinations imagined underworlds and other worlds, gods and suprahuman beings. Sadly, much of our western postmodern, post-everything culture looks downward not upward, accumulating grievances which must be compensated for or punished. For certain, the people living throughout the Fertile Crescent[5] were avid seekers of our beginnings. They labored intensely to understand who or what created us. This is one of many reasons I looked forward to our trip to Egypt, Yemen, Jordan, and Israel.

I was traveling, with stakeholders, as CEO of the Michigan charity that I was privileged to serve for ten years. The route of our first leg was from Chicago O'Hare to Frankfurt Main to Cairo International. While boarding, I was aware of a particularly noisy group of people who happen to settle on both sides of the two aisles around me in our wide-body A320. Even when traveling with others, I normally choose an aisle seat not adjacent to someone I know; excessive talkers drive me crazy so I avoid that risk. Other than reading, listening to music, or sleeping, it is highly likely that I will say very little, if anything, to the person seated next to me. Let's just say, as a seasoned traveler with a particular personality type, I get into my zone rather predictably.

"Sydney, I'm *starrr-ving*," said the loud female voice to my left. "I know, Sasha. Just hang on until we get in the air," said the male voice to my right, which I presumed to be of some relation. "But the food on planes is *so* bad," came the reply. "Can you please pass me the crackers?" Soon four passengers in between these rather irritating people had to pass a box overhead, one to the other, until the apparently ravenously hungry woman could be placated. It had only been a few months earlier I was in sub-Saharan Africa where hunger had a much different voice, punctuated by the cry of babies suffering from *kwashiorkor*, betrayed by the telltale sign of their swollen bellies.

With preflight announcements and videos of people unbuckling seat belts and sliding down inflatable rafts completed, I settled in for the eight-and-a-half-hour transatlantic flight. According to my travel journal I *did* grunt a hello to the European man sitting next to me. But now, with headphones on, I reviewed the details of our group itinerary and meeting details which I was singularly responsible for. I had regularly led groups of supporters in my charity work as CEO, and each time I tried to integrate visiting the field programs we support with some cultural sightseeing.

The connection and flight to Egypt was uneventful. As we approached, I stared at the brown, imposing Sahara Desert which stretched into the horizon for miles—3.55 million square miles, to be exact. Africa and the Arabian Peninsula are in a pitched battle from both north and south, as desertification from the Sahel, Kalahari, Namibian, and Arabian sands continually push to overtake the rich fertile tropical regions of this diverse and beautiful continent. Few people realize that Africa alone is larger than China, India, the contiguous US, and most of Europe *combined.*

We were met by our host, Dr. Mouneer from Harpour Memorial Hospital, who escorted us through the fashionable Heliopolis District, past the Citadel Mosque and Islamic Training Center, across the Qasr El Nil Bridge and eventually toward Giza. Checking into our Oberoi Hotel we were immediately awed by the awesome view of two of the three Giza Pyramids, with the third and the Sphinx just out of the line of sight. No sooner had we settled in than we heard the haunting voice of the *mouzeen* broadcast from the nearby minaret, calling the faithful to prayer, which in the Muslim faith occurs five times per day. This one, the *Salat al-mahgrib,* was the fourth, just after sunset.

After unpacking and freshening up we were treated to a traditional Egyptian meal of lamb kabob, fatteh, *kuesherie* (rice and lentils), and *umm ali* for dessert. Wally, our 6' 7" stockbroker, commented with every passing dish: "What is this?" "That smells interesting." "This looks weird." "Do you have any pizza?" We passed on (which is to say, declined) the water pipes which were generously located throughout the restaurant. Many patrons enjoyed this conversation-enhancing tradition. These colorful pipes seemed to be of particular interest to our amused giant. "Man, I could get use to this," he said with an impish grin. "Seems like everyone is bonging these days."

After a pleasant dinner we were shuttled to an outdoor seating area for the English version of the evening sound and light show with a stunning view of all three pyramids plus the Sphinx. The experience was nothing short of spectacular as we watched these ancient wonders of the world turn from powder blue to indigo and then bright yellow

Great Sphynx, Giza

to burnt sienna, accompanied by a clever blend of local traditional and western music. The Great Pyramid at Giza, also called the Pyramid of Khufu or Cheops, towers upward to 481 feet with one length of its base at 756 feet (or 440 Egyptian royal cubits) and a volume of 91 million cubic feet. Each layer of the more than five million total man-made blocks is made of carved limestone. These marvels, made by about 30,000 ancient masons over a period of twenty years, look incredibly like natural rock. They are the resting place of pharaohs and their possessions, yet the full contents throughout the labyrinth of many secret chambers are still unknown. And why were these built? The Egyptians were one of the first civilizations (like the Hebrews) who believed in an afterlife. *They* believed that a second self, the ka, lived within every human being. When the physical body expired, the ka enjoyed eternal life. Christians understand that *the great deceiver* has perpetually created false, alternative truths to the truth of Yahweh.[6]

Our purpose for being here was to bring material aid and assistance in support of multiple charitable initiatives. We promised Harpour Memorial Hospital a forty-foot container of medical supplies to be shipped following our visit; financial support to the Joint Refugee Ministry working with immigrants from Sudan; and much-needed equipment to a church clinic in Sadat City. We also inquired as to how we could best bring ecumenical help through the social services of the All Saints Cathedral.

Of course, *everyone always* wants to buy souvenirs, so we brought them to the fabled Khan el Khalili Bazaar. My small purchases were a beautiful lapis lazuli art piece and two rolled-up papyrus scrolls with classic Egyptian figures. Unlike my travel companions, I framed these

All Saints Cathedral, Cairo

at home, rather than lugging bulky items on and off planes with multiple countries still to travel to.

We rounded out our visit with a camel ride and a fascinating, marathon one-day trip to the ancient city of Thebes, modern-day Luxor. This was the ancient capital of the Upper Kingdom for more than a thousand years, with unimaginable wealth. Homer's *Iliad* said the wealth of Thebes was greater than the sands of the sea. Our Nubian guide was Gamal, whose name meant "handsome." He was also smart, working on his PhD in Egyptology. He was a wealth of valuable information. We took in all we could in this condensed time frame—Valley of the Kings, where sixty-two burial sites have been found included King Tut, Ramses, Queen Hatshepsut; as well as the massive Temples at Karnak—all the while downing ample bottles of water in the 40°C (110°F) heat. Memorable, to say the least. The next day we were off to the port city of Aden, Yemen via Asmara, Eritrea.

More recently, Aden has been heavily damaged by the Saudi-Yemeni conflict. In this time period Yemen was adopting a Western-style governmental system and had held its first direct presidential elections. We drove past multiple groups of squatting, turbaned men all chewing *qat*, which contains an alkaloid cathinone—a narcotic stimulant which keeps them buzzed all day long. We were there to provide medical supplies and assistance to the Ras Marbit Clinic, a Christ Church outpost in this intensely Muslim country. As Providence would have it, just four months later after our supplies arrived, this very clinic would be the one that served the sailors aboard the *USS Cole*. This guided missile destroyer had been bombed by al Qaeda while making a port call.

It was even hotter here than Luxor, so we asked for a quick dip in the Red Sea. Upon arriving we just stood and stared for a few uncomfortable seconds. Splashing in the hot water were a handful of men and a gaggle of noisy children. Seated on the burning sands of the beach were clusters of women in full black burqas with only a one-inch slit crossing over their eyes and a sliver of their nose. Muslim women living in these circumstances often face honor killings, polygamy, and lack of permission to do nearly anything without the expressed approval of her spouse or male family member. This is just the surface of their difficult circumstances.

Cloth shop Bab al Yemen

We made a quick overnight stop in Sana'a, the capital, with the group insisting that we visit the Bab al Yemen, a historic *souk* or market, in the heart of the city. Considered to have been originally designed by Shem the son of Noah, it received a facelift in the seventeenth century and is now open twenty-four hours a day. My only purchase was a *jambiya*, the distinctive curved and sheathed knife that all males to this day wear tucked in the front of their pants. A shower and a short night sleep at the Taj Sheba Hotel and we were off to Amman, Jordan.

With no time to first check into our hotel, we paid an official visit to HRH Prince Firas Bin Ra'ad at the Raghadan (working) Palace within the beautiful Royal Hashemite Court. There we offered to assist the Jordanian Sports Federation for the Handicapped with their children's program. Our main focus was to serve Christian relief ministries and youth camps. We have been particularly encouraged by the significant work being done through the indefatigable efforts of Isam Ghattas, now with his son Safa at his side, and their dedicated Manara Ministries team. This group fosters reconciliation amongst the kids at Camp Gilead attended by Muslims, Jews, and Christians. With always challenged resources, they make a valiant effort to meet the overwhelming needs from the crush of refugees coming to Jordan from Syria and throughout the region. I would encourage you to support this worthy organization with your donations and prayers.[7]

Next, I hired a tour company for our group to enjoy a jam-packed day in Israel, with stops in Jerusalem, Bethlehem, and Jericho. Our driver Majed took us out of the city of Amman past Bedouin tents, herding animals, and bare mountains. We crossed the King Hussein Bridge and completed a cumbersome border crossing which involved thorough baggage and body searches and lots of papers to stamp. We started our visit on the Mount of Olives, outside the walls of the Old City of Jerusalem.

Here we visited the gravesites of Haggai, Zechariah, and Malachi. Entering the East Gate, also called Lions Gate, we soon found ourselves on Via Dolarosa with its fourteen stations of the cross, shoulder to shoulder with tourists. We visited

Jerusalem

the Garden of Gethsemane, the Church of the Holy Sepulcher, and Golgotha—where my Lord was crucified.

After passing the Dome of the Rock mosque, built atop the Temple Mount site that has served as a symbol of faith for three religions for more than three thousand years, we went to the Wailing Wall.

Dome of the Rock / Temple Mount

For me, this was the absolute highlight. It was the anniversary of Israeli independence, and on this occasions non-Jews were allowed to enter. After sitting in a long queue our group was escorted to this holy place, with time allotted to pray. My journal recorded the moment: *I walked up to the wall with my head covered, leaned my head directly against the stones and prayed for ten minutes, emotion welling up. Along with a small folded written prayer we were able to push in between the stones of the wall, I prayed for peace, prayed for the future, and solemnly asked that God's will would be done on earth as it is in heaven. It was a moving and deeply meaningful experience.*

Our time outside Jerusalem began on Mount Nebo, where Moses looked over the Promised Land. We had a direct view of the Dead Sea, Jerusalem, and the Jordan River. As we drove down from our higher elevation, we passed a rugged area where Jesus is said to have been tempted in the wilderness. Then we came to a place marked "Bethany beyond the Jordan" where John the Baptist—the voice crying in the wilderness "prepare the way of the LORD; make straight in the desert a highway for our God" (Isa. 40:3)—fulfilled the prophecy of Isaiah and baptized Jesus. Every direction held significance. Over here Elisha was taken up into heaven. Over there Jesus met the woman at the well. History beckoning with 360-degree splendor.

Our final stop was Jericho. The large sign as we entered read, "The Oldest City in the World."

Human history on earth has only been recorded for about ten thousand years. God is eternal. Think about this! Our visit to this entire region was a reminder that the Creator of time and eternity came to us in the form of Jesus Christ, fully God and fully human—to whom every

Entering Jericho

knee shall bow and every tongue confess that He is Lord (Rom. 14:11).

Time has taken on a heightened importance as I have grown older. Every day is a gift. What have we done with *our* irreplaceable gift, our life, given to us with only a divinely allotted amount of time? My firstborn daughter died at age ten. My mother died at age ninety-two. The wick of every candle burns as it has been uniquely designed. Someday you and I will have passed into eternity. Yet now, while we still have breath, we must seize the opportunity to shine light into the darkness. It is important to remember that God's light is "continually short-circuited by the forces of evil in this world. . . . The sins of man . . . created a thunder cloud, as it were, that shut out the free shining of God's love. So, our Lord in the Garden of Gethsemane undertook the great work that we call atonement—the at-one-ment which reunited man with God . . . And as he was the Son of God and therefore able to transcend time, he took unto himself all of humanities sin, sickness, pain and death . . . past, present and future."[8]

Chapter 3
DOING VERSUS BEING

We are human beings, not human doings.
— **Deepak Chopra**

*W*ords are created for the first time when a new product, function, or experience becomes commonly understood and accepted. When we want to blow our nose, many people ask for a "Kleenex" instead of saying tissue. This makes the Kimberly-Clark people happy. When we need to do an internet search many of us say, "Google it." This makes the Bing and Yahoo people *not* happy.

For the more internationally acclimated, the terms "Balkanize" and "Balkanization" also have meaning. They are often considered pejorative geopolitical terms describing the process of fragmentation or division within a region or state into smaller regions or states, which are often hostile or uncooperative with one another. "Balkan" is a Turkish word meaning "mountain." The portion of Europe which is considered the Balkans—with many beautiful mountain ranges— includes Albania, Bosnia and Herzegovina, Bulgaria, Croatia, Kosovo, Montenegro, North Macedonia, Romania, Serbia, and Slovenia; before 1989, this list would have included Yugoslavia.

Much of the Balkans, previously under the geopolitical influence of the USSR until its disintegration, became realigned as new competing power structures and religious forces flourished. This precipitated centuries-old animosities, which blossomed unchecked into war and unimaginable suffering. It was for this reason that I committed to traveling to most of these countries for humanitarian purposes, multiple times over many years, to bring some hope and assistance. Our efforts amounted to a small life raft of relief in a sea of suffering people drowning in need.

Swiss Air to Zurich is always comfortable, but the continuing flight on Tarom Airlines to Bucharest, Romania was a grim portend of what awaited us. We arrived during the tumultuous months following the firing-squad execution of former Communist Party general secretary Nicolae Ceaușescu and his wife Elena. Fate allowed them a hasty trial, with a guilty verdict for genocide in their ordering the deaths of thousands of their own countrymen in Timișoara. For years, my friend and longtime traveling companion was Jack Henderson, MD. I am quite certain that no other person spent more time with me on the road. "Dr. Jack," as he is affectionately called, extended the mercy of Jesus with a clear-eyed practicality and nonjudgmental affirmation, not to mention a keen sense of humor. He had served as a pediatrician for most of his career and now played a valuable role in our medical programs. Together we touched many people, both physically and spiritually.

The ripple effect of the fall of the Soviet Empire massively impacted the Balkans. The septic reaction to a gangrenous amputated leg brought an end to communist revolutionary and "President" Josip Tito of the former Yugoslavia. Enver Hoxha, first secretary of the Party of Labour of Albania, allegedly had a nervous breakdown and committed suicide. Todor Zhivkov, general secretary of the Bulgarian Communist Party, as well as a rogue's gallery of other dictators, each faded into infamy. Their departures ushered in a troubled period of post-authoritarianism like a woman in hard labor. The world had just watched in horror as an ABC television exposé revealed thousands of children warehoused in dirty, run down "orphanages."

"Jack," I said, "We have an extremely compact schedule this time. I'm sorry."

As always, his response was gracious. "As long as we accomplish what we came for, I am with you all the way."

As we drove through gray and dingy Bucharest our first stop was the Centrul Budimex Hospital, in urgent need of pediatric and orthopedic equipment and supplies, among many other items. Our focus was on the children. We met with the State Secretary for the Handicapped to get the official version of the condition of this country's health services for children, particularly special needs kids. It is one thing to record facts and statistics or listen to rote lectures on mortality and morbidity rates; it is quite another dimension of human empathy to see, hear, and hold the precious little ones whom God loves more than we can comprehend.

Thus, our journey of ghoulish discovery began in earnest. In the village of Voluntari we visited "Special School #10" for boys—a run-down, poorly staffed, and dirty facility with adolescent boys running undisciplined throughout the facility.

Flying northeast to Cluj we visited the Spitalul Clinic de Recuperare (rehabilitation hospital). In Ceaușescu's macabre worldview,

children were wards of the state and, as such, had an obligation to contribute to Romania's global image. Rigorous and intensely demanding state-run sports training programs were set up to produce national heroes like Nadia Comăneci, the first Olympic athlete to score a perfect ten in gymnastics. Many talented athletes were developed. But the dark underbelly of this myopic system created hundreds of "orphanages," filled with children who were

Romanian orphan   intentionally set aside from public view.

These underfunded and understaffed facilities housed some children who legitimately had no parents. Many more, in desperate times, were abandoned by parents on the doorsteps of these ubiquitous children's nightmares. What was much worse, and grievously unfair, were the thousands of children with minor physical irregularities or learning disabilities who were classified by the state as "irrecuperable." Translation: incapable of succeeding in their national sports training gulag. Thus, these precious children were abandoned to a heartless system of neglect.

We visited *so* many young boys and girls in facilities across the country—greater Bucharest, Cluj, Iași, Suceava, Oradea, Constanța, and more. We entered one facility that will never be erased from my memory. I asked, "Jack, look at these beautiful young children in these decrepit cribs. They are rocking back and forth on their knees. Why is that?"

Dr. Jack looked at me soberly while explaining his diagnosis. "This is one of the seven telltale signs of abuse or neglect. These children *need* to be loved, touched, and held."

"Oh my God, Jack, this is so sad!" I blurted out as I lifted eight-year-old Sofia, who buried her head into my neck just above my shoulder. I hugged her, with tears streaming down my face, for nearly five minutes. Katya, with a speech impediment, was too shy or afraid to be picked up so I just put my hand through the rusty metal support structure of her crib, with *no* mattress, and simply held her hand. She was looking away, but slowly turned her head then grabbed my hand with her two little ones. "Dear God," I prayed with a lump in my throat, "Please show us how best to bring your light into this dark place." Any significant intervention would require a detailed plan and strategy for raising the money.

Besides sending material aid to many of these facilities, we were able to help launch a national kinetotherapy association with formal ties to a major American physical therapy company.[1] They created a vacation bank where employees donated a certain number of days from their accrued vacations, enabling the company to send a rotation of two-person therapist teams to work with the poorly trained Romanian staff. Over time they made a lasting and tangible improvement in the well-being of these precious children.

We started our journey west toward Hungary, first securing tickets on an overnight sleeper train. Our journey brought us through the Carpathian Mountains into the heart of Transylvania, where so many stories grew into fables and legends. While the click-clack of the wheels massaged our fatigue, we passed quaint villages, picturesque farms, sawmills, pigs, chickens, and women with babushka scarves who carried loads fit for a mule. At one two-hour stretch, as the train stopped in a few towns and villages to pick up more passengers, we crowded into one "day car" with pull-down benches for six, and listened mesmerized as our Romanian-American friends Cornel and Elena, now living in the Amish/Mennonite area of east-central Ohio, told us their story. Facing hunger, harassment, despair, and imprisonment for being Christians who did not deny their faith, they finally escaped. It took multiple dangerous attempts in the dark of night over four years for them to succeed. In the end, dependence on God and an underground network of sympathizers and discreet people of faith provided the means.

This was my closing journal entry on this leg of one trip: *I am in awe of the suffering church. We will never know the price people have paid for their faith. Freedom is most valued when it has not always been available. I perceive America is slipping away from this poignant truth. Lord have mercy on us.*

It makes you feel good when you have done something for someone in need. There is value to both persons in the interaction. I avoid using the terms *giver* and *receiver* because my overwhelming experience is that, in God's design, there is intentional and mutual benefit in doing something tangible. *Doing* is a means to love one another in continuous fulfillment of the Great Commandment. Scripture clearly admonishes us to be doers of the word and not hearers only—that we will be blessed in our doing. Another passage describes the Son of Man coming with his angels to judge the nations, explaining our reward for giving food to someone who is hungry, drink to the thirsty, clothing to the naked, caregiving for the sick, hospitality to the stranger, and visits to those in prison (Matt. 25:35–36). Of course, this is a representative, not exhaustive, list of acts of mercy and compassion. God created us for relationship, for us to be with him and with each other, and that love should permeate his entire creation.

Most of us will agree that one of the most prominent contemporary *saints* who "did" more for the poor than almost anyone was Mother Teresa. She was born Anjezë Bojaxhiu, in Skopje, North Macedonia to Albanian and Indian parents. I vividly remember her death September 5, 1997, because it was just five days after the horrific high-speed car accident on August 31, 1997 where Princess Diana passed into eternity. I was in a hotel room somewhere in Asia and remember the nonstop coverage on BBC. Two brilliant lights in a dark world.

After her death, Teresa was beatified in 2003 as Saint Teresa of Calcutta. When she took her final vows in 1937 before starting her ministry, she proclaimed that she would become "the spouse of Jesus for all eternity." Mother Teresa established the Missionaries of Charity, dedicated to the service of the poorest of the poor. Returning to India and residing temporarily with the Little Sisters of the Poor she went for the first time to the slums. She visited families, washed the sores of children, and cared for an old dying man lying sick with hunger and tuberculosis. She dedicated the remainder of her life to serve "amongst the unwanted, the unloved and the uncared for."[2] This saint served God *both* in her doing *and* in her being. Scripture has many examples to remind us that God intimately and thoroughly knows our heart, our secrets, our motivations—which is why just *doing* does not complete the fullness of God's purpose for us.

For some of us there can be a flip side to "doing." It can become an end to itself instead of a means to something greater, and has the potential to breed a false sense of pride. *Look what I am doing.* I'm thankful that early in my faith commitment to Jesus at age nineteen, I learned the value of journaling. These are some of my reflections: *In my schedule I am always moving, traveling, doing. I've spent much of my life busy doing something. . . . Eventually I realized that my periodic exhaustion was unnecessary. Regrettably, some of my strivings and doings lacked eternal value.*

One of the best writings on the importance of being and not just doing comes from a book coauthored by my friend Don Ankenbrandt, *210 Project: Discover Your Place in God's Story.* His chapter, which hits the nail on the head, is titled "Identity: Who You Are, Not What You Do." Over a lifetime, "many voices in our lives shape our view of the world, of ourselves, of others and of God. . . . The single most important battle in your life is the battle over who you are."[3] God created us for a purpose. We were created to be in relationship with Him and for something significant. True saints live with a powerful presence of God that reaches beyond their physical, tangible service. You can *feel* that essence in who they *are* and what they *do.*

Back to my journal: *I was listening to some old hymns on a "Best of" CD when the choir starting to sing "Sweet Hour of Prayer." Are you kidding me? Pray for one hour! But, YES, that is my desire . . . to be in the overwhelming presence of God.* Then some months later: *A profound revelation this morning during my quiet time—accompanied by a strong sense of the presence of the Holy Spirit. Love is all that lasts. "Being" means living and expressing love to all. I need to love those that God puts in my path whether I "do" anything for them or not.* A similar passage, from a devotional book, has also brought me profound encouragement:

Rest in Me. When tired nature rebels it is her call for rest. Rest then until My Life Power flows through you. Have no fear for the future. Be quiet, be still, and in that very stillness your strength will come and will be maintained. The world sees strength in action. In My Kingdom it is known that strength lies in quiet. "In quietness and in confidence shall be your strength." Such a promise! Such glorious fulfillment! The strength of Peace and the Peace of strength. Rest in Me. Joy in Me.[4]

No travel summary in the Balkans would be complete without a brief explanation of the inherent evil from two destructive wars which raged in the region from 1992–1999.

Back to our destination. Sarajevo, Yugoslavia had hosted the fourteenth Winter Olympics in February 8–19, 1984—beating out contenders Sapporo, Japan and Gotheburg, Sweden—and venue sites from their history were still present, though run down. This naturally beautiful city is nestled in a valley surrounded by the Dinaric Alps, situated along the Miljacka River in the heart of the Balkans. We launched this particular visit, one of many, from Split, Croatia on the spectacular Dalmatian coast of the Adriatic. Our group was larger this time, including gospel singer Allison Speer and husband Brian, photojournalist extraordinaire Jerry Kitchel, financial supporters, and, of course, Dr. Jack.

The Roman emperor Diocletian had built his massive third-century palace here, which beckons the lover of history to explore. However, Diocletian must also be vilified for the Great Persecution—the decree putting to death innumerable Christians of this era. Nero banned Christianity, but Diocletian did his best to eradicate it. And yet, juxtaposed to the palace is a quiet symbol of God's salvation history, the Cathedral of Saint Domnius. Built in 305 AD, it is considered the oldest cathedral in the world. The true church, the bride of Christ, will *never* be eradicated. If you ever plan to visit this region, include a drive along the crystalline coastline from Split to Dubrovnik a four-and-a-half-hour trip by car. But *do* stop along the way; it's so beautiful. And, *yes*, you *can* get a banana split in Split!

The historic part of our trip included a visit to the renown Međugorje, a holy pilgrimage site for many Catholics who travel there hoping to view a current apparition of the "Virgin Mary Queen of Peace" which was said to have first occurred in 1981. How desperately this region needed the hope of this place in this post-war period.

As our rented ten-passenger van wound through snow-filled mountains toward Sarajevo it took twice as long as anticipated. We had to stop multiple times behind UN relief supply truck convoys putting chains on their tires. Others were winching themselves out of ditches in the slippery snow and slush. Once our van slid sideways, dangerously close to an eighty-foot drop-off. We all got out, except for the driver, of course, to push.

UN trucks deliver aid

We reached the mountain pass surrounding this war-damaged capital, and then headed down the muddy, potholed access highway into the seat of authority for what is now called Bosnia and Herzegovina.

The Holiday Inn, at that time, was the least damaged place we could stay. My journal recorded these impressions: *Everything is blown out including this Holiday Inn. The entire front side of this ten-story facility is pock marked with shrapnel and bullet holes. Upwards of half the rooms are not functional as evidenced by the blackened interiors. We checked in at a temporary folding table and climbed stairs to our rooms. Hallways are lit by a single, uncovered incandescent lightbulb with every third socket working. Brian and Allison's window is taped over with plywood. Mine has glass but won't close completely, and it's cold outside.* We learned later that snipers still occupied some buildings just across the square from our hotel. My constant companion, my journal, proclaimed, *Danger is all around, but so are God's angels.*

Our itinerary was jammed. First, we visited necessary government ministries, reemerging after being shut down by the war, to learn the general lay of the land. We touched base with multiple international charities (sometimes called nongovernmental organizations, or NGOs) and visited most of the larger hospitals. This may seem like a simple process. It was not. Many times, we had to pass through five or six checkpoints controlled by various IFOR military units, short for Implementation Force. This was the NATO-led multinational peacekeeping conglomerate made up of military units from thirty-two countries, which did their best to control the still raw and fractious environment. With our US passports Dr. Jack and I were able to visit with the US Command.

We secured a most important interview with LTC Mark D. from Florida, the public affairs officer and an outspoken Christian, who directed us to some particular places of need. With a hired driver, translator, and a roster of key contacts we set out to listen and to serve.

With Dr. Jack in Bosnia

Our visits to faith groups exceeded in meaning and importance anything we could have imagined. A local church-based clinic was comprised of four contiguous twenty-foot shipping containers, with a passage cut between them. Dr. K had three children in pain: one-year-old Ivan has a bad earache; eight-month old Puce with spina bifida had an upper-respiratory infection; and Amar, who looked to be about ten going on twenty, had cut himself on concertina wire, placed seemingly everywhere.

We drove along Dragon of Bosnia Street, crudely referred to as "Sniper Alley," the main commercial district. During the war, Serb snipers were deployed by Slobodan Milosevic, referred to as "The Butcher of the Balkans"; Milosevic was later brought to trial at The Hague for genocide and war crimes, astoundingly ending without a verdict. Snipers who had perched in the higher elevations would pick off teenagers who volunteered for their families to run to the food stores which stayed open after midnight—*because* they could run faster.

We met Nikola, who was married during the war and had spent his honeymoon with his frightened bride, surrounded by the crossfire of soldiers at every major intersection. Over a period of seven days, eighteen of their closest friends and family were killed. Can you fathom the emotional trauma this created in them? Nikola looked at us and said with profound simplicity, "People must find a new power: the power to forgive."

As one writer described the region, "The sleeping beasts of Balkan ethnicity had been unleashed. While Bosnia did have one sophisticated urban center where Croats, Serbs, Muslims, and Jews had traditionally lived together in reasonable harmony, the villages all around were full of savage hatreds, leavened by poverty and alcoholism."[5]

A local pastor guided us to the Musa Family. Stephanic was currently unemployed but well-skilled. His wife, a recent convert from Islam, and their five children lived in a converted shipping container, as did many of their neighbors, sometimes in combined family groups.

Brian and Allison blessed them with a cash gift, and we left them school kits and supplies for baby Senada, their youngest daughter.

Our journey of mercy took us to many other places. In the snowy mountains of Tuzla, we learned of the massacre of seventy-one students, and two hundred more with serious injuries. We visited Gradina Hospital and many health clinics, promising aid. We even attended the Protestant chapel at the invitation of chaplain Lee T. in the fortified US military compound. Signs everywhere read, "Warning: Landmines." The other sign that caught our attention declared, "Tuzla Chapel—Blessed are the Peacemakers."

In the devastated city of Mostar (which means "bridge") we visited USAID, the US embassy, and multiple humanitarian centers. We took a vote of our group and unanimously agreed to each shoulder one twenty-five-pound box of food or supplies and hike about one mile up a steep mountain with snow up to our thighs, to deliver food to a lovely Christian family in a homemade log cabin-type dwelling. They were overwhelmed with surprise and gratitude.

The evening service at Mostar Evangelical Church simultaneously broke our hearts and lifted them up again. We entered the small, cold, sparsely furnished room, with every square inch filled with young and old alike singing lively Christian choruses. Vinka's testimony which followed was riveting,

Mostar Bridge, Bosnia

told with clear recall but without emotion. She shared how she barely missed being killed by a grenade which threw her across the room of her flat; sadly, her brother *was* killed. She told us of a recurring dream where almost nightly she obsessed about one onion. In the dream she would repeatedly put this one onion in a pot of boiling water, salivating about the imagined flavor. For weeks all she had for a meal was hot water and a few crackers. Already slender, she had lost an additional twenty pounds. When she ran out of food, and not having younger family members, she would steal out in the eerie night to get a few basic staples, never sure if she would make it back alive. She looked at us, concluding, "What good is gold in war when you have nothing to eat?"

Following a nonverbal sign from Pastor Kormelo, this vibrant community of believers began to sing the theme song from the movie *The Hiding Place*,[6] followed by the Hallelujah Chorus. At this moment, we were in a holy place graced by the presence of God. I was asked to bring "a word," and I shared some thoughts from Romans 8. Then Allison blessed the grateful congregation with a few numbers from her *Cross of Christ* CD. The central portion of the service was pastor's sermon from Revelation 2 which included an emphasis on verse 3—which only the suffering church gathered with us could fully understand: "You have persevered and have endured hardships for my name, and have not grown weary."

We all agreed that this trip had changed our lives. Our understanding. Our faith. My final journal entry was a series of bullet points attempting to sort out the jumble of feelings pressing in on my chest:

- *God, why?*
- *War is such stupidity. Nothing is worth this agony.*
- *Pain everywhere. I feel so moved with compassion. Lord, use us to bring healing, hope.*
- *We didn't expect this to happen to us!*

- *"In their dark night of war, faith had become a living flame."*[7]
- *So many stories told to us with calm, but with a far-away look in their eyes, cold silent suffering.*
- *If you went out for bread you didn't know if you'd come home alive. My God!*
- *Hope is an ember that lives eternally in the Lord's people.*
- *I have a trip to South Korea in two weeks. Father, give me strength.*

Chapter 4

WISDOM OR KNOWLEDGE

It is the province of knowledge to speak, and it is the privilege of wisdom to listen.
— ***Oliver Wendell Holmes***

ne of my favorite international films is *The Gods Must Be Crazy*. It was the highest grossing South African-produced film ever, at $200 million worldwide. A comedy that kept you laughing from start to finish, it follows the story of Xi, a San[1] farmer from the Ju/'Hoansi bushmen in the Kalahari Desert of Botswana who have no knowledge of the world beyond. One day, a glass Coca-Cola bottle is carelessly thrown out of an open window by the pilot of a small airplane passing overhead. It falls to the sand below, unbroken. At first, they consider this strange artifact a "gift" from the gods, as they also considered the plants and animals. But this unusual arrival appears to create unforeseen conflict. After much discussion they decide to make a pilgrimage to the edge of the world to dispose of this cursed thing.

The plot twists and turns as Xi sets out on this journey. For me, one line was immortalized. A PhD researcher, Dr. Andrew Steyn, headed to this region to study manure samples in different species, stops at his last watering hole before heading into the bush. While seated at the bar, he looks over at the man next to him and asks, "Is the noise in my head bothering you?" Eventually he meets up with Xi and they both contribute their *knowledge* of the world around them to a lighthearted conclusion.

Let's start with a simple, partial definition: "Knowledge applies to any body of facts gathered by study, observation, or experience."[2] Yet, what we consider to be knowledge is an elusive mist. Knowledge seldom stays the same forever. Even when applying our contemporary scientific method,[3] "facts" derived from observation, establishing a question, forming a hypothesis, making a prediction and testing the prediction . . . may change.

For example, in early human history the practice of "trepanning" or "trepanation" was performed. This was a medical procedure to drill a hole into the cranium of a person who was behaving in what was considered an abnormal way. The procedure allegedly released what practitioners of the day believed were evil spirits. Pythagoras and the Greeks discovered the mathematical means to determine that the earth was a sphere and not flat. Germs causing viruses were discovered in the 1890s. Before this, other *knowledge* was used to determine the origin of diseases. Today, when we read or listen to the "news" in *any* media platform, what many consider facts, as reported, are far from that! And what of our bushman, Xi and his *knowledge* of the Coke bottle? For that matter, what about us? What do we cling to as factual knowledge? Most often, perception is reality. Everything we believe to be true is screened through our own life experience and understanding of the world around us. That essentially makes us the arbiters of truth— unless we seek a higher truth.

It has taken me decades to understand that the more I know, the less I know. Which is to say, as we learn more, we discover new vistas and worlds of knowledge that were previously unknown to us. Does knowledge make us "smart"? People walk around like zombies fixated on "smart" phones. Go figure. And then consider the role of formal education in the acquisition of knowledge. I know some highly degreed people who lack common sense, practical knowledge. I've met illiterates with minimal formal education, in countries where I have served, who *know* more about life than most of us. Some people think that learning takes place during a period of life, when in fact it should be a *way* of life. Lifelong learning is a gift that never ceases.

Who is the smartest person you've ever known? Do you feel that way because he or she can explain how to factor a complex mathematical equation or expand on some other body of knowledge? Or is it because that person helped you understand something more impactful and vital to living, such as why lack of forgiveness is poison for your soul?

Most major faith groups believe God is all-knowing. In my own faith journey, I have discovered that when I pray, God *is* in my heart, not just out there somewhere. But he *is* out there as well. Now, when I pray, I seldom jabber at him with my requests. Instead, I have learned to listen more intently to the wisdom of the ages. There is another dynamic to consider if we only seek knowledge:

> For the foolishness of God is wiser than human wisdom, and the weakness of God is stronger than human strength. Brothers and sisters, think of what you were when you were called. Not many of you were wise by human standards; not many were influential; not many of noble birth. But God chose the foolish things of the world to shame the wise; God chose the weak things of the world to shame the strong. God chose the lowly things of this world and the despised things—and the things that are not—to nullify the things that are, so that no one may boast before him. It is because of him that you are in Christ Jesus, who has become for us wisdom from God. **(1 Cor. 1:25–30)**

Wisdom is *far* more valuable than knowledge. The Bible has *much* to say about wisdom, particularly the collection of books called wisdom literature comprised of Job, Psalms, Proverbs, Ecclesiastes, and Song of Songs. "Where then does wisdom come from? Where does understanding dwell? It is hidden from the eyes of every living thing. . . . God understands the way to it and he alone knows where it dwells, for he views the ends of the earth and sees everything under the heavens" (Job 28:20–21, 23–24).

Elijah was speaking with God on Mount Horeb, explaining what God already knew—that the Israelites had rejected his covenant, torn down his altars, and put to death his prophets. They were now trying to kill him. In response, the Lord instructed Elijah, "'Go out and stand on the mountain in the presence of the Lord, for the Lord is about to pass by.' Then a great and powerful wind tore the mountains apart and shattered the rocks before the LORD, but the LORD was not in the wind. After the wind there was an earthquake, but the Lord was not in the earthquake. After the earthquake came a fire, but the LORD was not in the fire. And after the fire came a gentle whisper. When Elijah heard it, he pulled his cloak over his face" (1 Kings 19:11–13). He knew in his spirit that he was hearing directly from the Creator of the Universe.

How do we hear God? Most often, when alone, it is in quiet meditation that we enter his presence. Then he will reveal wisdom and give discernment. "And he said to the human race, 'The fear of the LORD—that is wisdom, and to shun evil is understanding'" (Job 28:28); "Teach us to number our days, that we may gain a heart of wisdom" (Ps. 90:12).

For two-thirds of my career I served as president/CEO of two charities in succession and a small medical products company; therefore, my stories come from this orientation. In the world of humanitarian work, during times of severe societal disruption, collaborative global engagement is needed. Man-made conflicts such as war, civil unrest, and the mass migration of refugees or internally displaced persons are in one category. The other category includes famine, epidemics (such as

Ebola), other health crises (such as HIV/AIDS), and natural disasters of all types. These two categories of crises are the twin sisters of human suffering. Unlike program staff who deliver services or specialists who bring unique skills, my role as a CEO has been to be a voice of advocacy to communicate the need, as well as a conduit to secure the resources to meet those needs. That is why being in a crisis or emergency situation, in the earliest stages of assessment and program start up is important. I had the privilege of presenting my nonacademic paper on Disaster Response Teams (DRTs) to the United Nations at the Palais des Nations in Geneva, Switzerland. In the context of a DRT I would have served as team leader. Other team members included a logistician, epidemiologist, communications officer, and others, depending on the specific situation. When launching a humanitarian program, we often employed this model.

One of my favorite countries on the planet is South Africa. I love that place . . . the beauty despite the pain. The story which follows emphasizes my global role—as a voice and a conduit, an ambassador if you will, between those who have and those who have something different.

I was privileged to have met former President F. W. de Klerk here in the US when we invited him to be the keynote speaker at one of our annual banquets. His role in history is a fascinating one. In 1990 he released Nelson Mandela from Victor Verster Prison on Robben Island, 13.9 kilometers from Cape Town, in the raucous waters of Table Bay where the Atlantic and Indian oceans converge. *Robben* is a Dutch word for "seals," which are ubiquitous in the Cape region. Mr. Mandela had spent eighteen of his twenty-seven years behind bars in this isolated place, also a UNESCO World Heritage Site. He had a full view of beautiful Table Mountain which overshadows Cape Agulhas, the southernmost point on the regal continent of Africa.

Through a series of negotia-
tions, these two notable men determined the unilateral steps tak-
en by the de Klerk government
to dismantle apartheid. This
led to the first multiracial election of Mandela and his African
National Congress party in 1994.

Table Mountain, Cape Town

The ANC has won each successive election, which occurs every five
years. For this peaceful transition out of apartheid, both men were
awarded the Nobel Peace Prize. In November 2019, when the South
African Springboks defeated England 12–32 in the quadrennial Rugby
World Cup, I sent an email to my now longtime friend F. W., who responded within twenty-four hours with appreciation and thanks, rep-
resenting every celebrating citizen of this resilient country.

Our itinerary, as always, included assessment of the humanitarian
needs we would support. But unlike most trips, this one included
many more business contacts, in a concerted effort to network with the
leaders of companies and foundations which comprise the economic
base in greater southern Africa. Our goal was to secure charitable
donations. Two American businessmen accompanied me, one who had
been posted here with Goodyear for more than a decade. Of the many
great locations to stay in Cape Town, I prefer the old colonial charm
of the Vineyard Hotel in the southern suburb of Newlands, fairly close
to the University of Cape Town. We started with a networking day to
secure important personal introductions and connections.

Driving on the N1 north to Paarl we pulled up to the gated eighty-
five-hectare private farm of F. W. and his wife Elita in Wildepaardejacht,
which is Afrikaans for "wild horses running." They were gracious as
always, particularly since they had just returned from Europe where
they had attended a black-tie gala for Nobel laureates. Our invitation

began with lunch including one of the Cloete family, among the most prominent in Cape Town. With a marvelous array of healthy selections and ample South African wine, we listened to tales involving the mayor of Rome, the crown prince of (the former) Yugoslavia, King Constantine of Greece, former Soviet president Mikhail Gorbachev, and others. And, as generously offered by Mr. de Klerk, we also secured key contact information for many business and political movers and shakers.

F.W. and Elita de Klerk

Keeping an eye on his watch F.W. announced, "Alright gentlemen, it's time to prepare for our golf game." Always the humorous one, I responded, "I will be ecstatic if I break one hundred." That secured a raised eyebrow from our host. As we drove to the Boschenmeer Golf Estates we were joined by a bodyguard—I assume every former president of a country has at least one! My friend Bud Hoffman got to ride shotgun in the golf cart with F.W. and continued to receive valuable contacts for our follow-up.

Golf with F.W.

After an enjoyable afternoon in this idyllic setting we returned to extend our thanks, take some photos, and pay a fond farewell to both de Klerks. As we headed back, we passed picturesque Somerset West, the spectacular Cape Winelands in beautiful Stellenbosch, and Franschhoek Valley which we had visited previously. After the briefest time to freshen up we were off to a fabulous seafood dinner on the Victoria and Alfred Waterfront. The remainder of our Cape Town journey involved this two-track purpose: locate financial sources and persons of influence, and determine where we would invest these funds when they were secured. Our itinerary reflected the stark dichotomy between the hard-earned but comfortable life and living conditions of most of the Dutch and English world in South Africa and the black and mixed-race world, which lived with undeserved restrictions and multidimensional suffering.

In our sincere desire to honor God and serve those in need, we visited many health and humanitarian sites to assess our capacity to help. The needs were staggering: Christian Community Association and clinic for the deaf; Groote Schuur Hospital—home of "the surgeon who dared," Dr. Christiaan Barnard, who successfully conducted the first human-to-human heart transplant; Rehoboth Center for the Aged; St. Luke's Hospital in the impoverished Cape Flats. Then with locally recognized community leaders as our guides and caution-keepers, we visited the Haut Bay squatter settlement of Imizamo Yethu; Langa, the oldest black township in the Cape—"a forgotten community"; the Khayelitsha slums; the oppressed Gugulethu township; and Hanover Park, one of the most violent places in the region.

Now we set out in earnest to locate sources of funding and collaborative partnerships. We took a memorable trip, traveling northeast on the N2 in the bright African sun. We passed spectacular flora and fauna along the Garden Route in the Eastern Cape headed to Port Elizabeth, dubbed both the Windy City and the Friendly City. Continuing on the N2, we made strategic stops to potential donors referred to us in the seaside communities of Knysna and Plettenberg Bay. We made a most pleasant stop at the "Heads," a narrow slip in the mountain where the forceful Indian Ocean comes in at high tide to fill a vast inland lake. We also briefly toured Tsitsikamma National Park, and later watched the surfers on Jeffries and St. Francis Bays.

This trip, too, was a rare gastronomical delight, including Blackbeard's Tavern serving fresh calamari, lobster, and prawns just caught fresh on the fishing boats within site of the shore. We made the best haul of contacts at an invitation-only affair at the St. George's Club. Built in 1901, this classic colonial "gentlemen's club" sported framed art of patrons, sailing ships, and hunting dogs. We were introduced to senior officers and some CEOs of banks, foundations, and companies of various sizes. It was a slice of life my accompanying business associates were comfortable with, but one in which I was unaccustomed. Our evening started with drinks and hors d'oevres in the bar, followed by a multiple-course meal in the dining room at white-clothed tables with name placards. We slowly worked our way through a two-hour meal, with even more selections of wine.

After all the good humor, talking, and connecting we "retired" to private chambers for an aperitif and cigars for those who indulged. I remarked, "At home, most of my meals are a utilitarian necessity eaten rather quickly." Our new friends, Brian and his wife Anne, retorted almost simultaneously, "Here in South Africa meals are a journey." Instantly, my mind drifted to the squatter camps and shanty towns I had visited, where the daily existence was a much different reality. *How long, Lord, until all the people of this amazing country can go to sleep in peace with a full stomach, and an opportunity to succeed and prosper?*

Our final stops were in the Sandton district of Johannesburg, and then Praetoria. With the introductions made for us by Mr. de Klerk and other influencers, we met with the US ambassador to South Africa, just returned from Helsinki, as well as chairmen of The Business Bank, D. G. Murray Trust, G. A. Foundation, Delta Foundation, the Rotary, Satchi & Satchi, Warner-Lambert Pharmaceuticals, Weyth, Eli Lilly, 3M, Johnson & Johnson, Royal Dutch Shell, AMCHAM (American Chamber of Commerce), Angloval Mining, and others.

Over the years now, I have raised an aggregate of about $2.3 billion in combined cash and "gifts-in-kind" (GIK). For US tax purposes GIK refers to donated products, including manufactured goods, which are beneficial to the corporate donor as a tax write-off. Major companies also have CSR funds—corporate social responsibility money available to invest in local community projects. Then, of course, there are many public and private grants available if one knows where to find them. It is also a core principle of development to connect wealthy individuals who have a specific philanthropic bent toward compatible initiatives. It is said that money follows passion, not the other way around. A key to effective fundraising is understanding what your potential donor is passionate about. I have always felt schizophrenic in the global humanitarian world in which I have passionately engaged for decades. It seems I am always careening into danger, poverty, sickness, and sadness—while tapping on the metaphorical shoulders of the well-heeled to get them to see the suffering right under their noses. It is a delicate dance. These were notes from my journal:

> *It has been a fulfilling trip, challenging the senses with beauty and piercing the heart with a deep desire to help. It is vital that we support mobilizing the community of faith. Without God in the equation, hearts are not permanently changed. In post-apartheid South Africa, we were told—by black and white alike—of pervasive tribalism, stifling illiteracy, grinding poverty, massive unemployment, rampant HIV and STDs, shocking crime rate, political turmoil, severe graft and corruption, severe child sexual abuse, rape, alcoholism, and violence. Sustainable solutions are most often found in communities of faith, and rarely achieved by political action.*

Bidding a fond farewell to my traveling companions I flew 6,784 kilometers north to Addis Ababa, capital of Ethiopia. My assignment was to teach two intensive courses through Azusa Pacific University as a part of their Operation Impact initiative. As a subject matter specialist with a doctorate, I was assigned students enrolled in their master of arts program in organizational leadership degree program. My course was "Current Issues in Leadership." The first week was in the capital Addis, with two dozen bright, emerging leaders on the launch point of their professional careers. Besides a full day of class presentation, we shared daily insights and assignments, group breakout sessions, book reviews, and a post-course research paper focused on an individualized area of interest fully germane to the existing context of leadership needs in Ethiopia. I benefitted as much, if not more, from these wonderful students than they did from me.

The second intensive week was in the smaller city of Awassa, 278 kilometers south. My students were all government officials and equally interested, but much more inhibited in their group interactions. Sometimes I would ask an open-ended question for discussion and hear crickets. It is an axiom of life, or at least my observation of it, that the older we get the more reticent we become. Over time, outside influences and the pressure to conform make us less comfortable functioning outside the expected norm. We call this enculturation. And for immigrants in a new land, another phenomenon may occur— acculturation, which is assimilation to a different culture, usually the dominant one. When teaching leadership principles, understanding these nuances is very important.

Toward the end of this longer than usual trip I was tired and ready to go home. On my last night I lay under my mosquito netting in the now-familiar humidity listening to downpouring rain. In the morning I received a message from British Air that their food service workers at London Heathrow went out on strike, so I had to scramble for another route home. With some unexpected good fortune, I was successfully rebooked and bumped up to business class at no charge. I thanked God for this welcomed blessing. I had a family that needed me and it was time to be back home.

Of all the literature of the ages, that seeks knowledge and considers wisdom, I want to share one very simple reflection at an ephemeral, human level:

> *We measure our weight and tally our steps. Every day we stare at a screen, press buttons and count, but we don't count what really counts, our moments together. We'll never know how many chances we'll get to gather by the ocean under a blue sky. Or make the best of a rainy day. How many chances will we have to dance or forgive or break the awkward silence with a joke. How many opportunities will there be to pack our bags and embark on an adventure? Sometimes we forget that the things that count most are those that can't be counted.*[4]

Chapter 5

FATHERHOOD

> *No man can possibly know what life means, what the world means, what anything means, until he has a child and loves it.*
> — ***Koizumi Yakumo, aka Lafcadio Hearn***

God is spirit (John 4:24), not flesh, and neither male nor female as we understand human gender. Genesis teaches us that God created humanity male and female in his[1] image and likeness (Gen. 1:27). We are divinely separated into male and female, wholly complementary, distinct but equal, and mutually valued and loved by our Creator. Unlike the other heavenly hosts of his creation, we were given the power to procreate. Since he made us this way, it has always been part of his created order that a child needs the nurture, guidance, and discipline of a father *and* a mother. The spiritually discerning understand that our deceitful adversary seeks to steal, kill, and destroy (John 10:10) *all* that God has created to be good.

It should come as no surprise then that fathers, fatherhood, the traditional family, and traditional roles and responsibilities have been, since the beginning of time, under attack. Today especially, this onslaught has taken on new virulence and violence. There are current political movements advocating for the cessation of the nuclear family, while others have created an alphabet soup of alleged new gender categories.

50

More level-headed assessment has come from both sides of the political divide. "There is a father absence crisis in America. According to the U.S. Census Bureau, 19.7 million children, more than 1 in 4, live without a father in the home. Consequently, there is a father factor in nearly all social ills facing America today."[2] On June 15, 2008 then-Senator Barack Obama made a speech to the Apostolic Church of God in Chicago, with these notable comments:

> *Of all the rocks upon which we build our lives, we are reminded today that the family is the most important. And we are called to recognize and honor how critical every father is to that foundation. But if we are honest with ourselves, we'll admit that what too many fathers are . . . missing from too many lives and too many homes . . . children who grow up without a father are five times more likely to live in poverty and commit crime; nine times more likely to drop out of schools and twenty times more likely to end up in prison. They are more likely to have behavioral problems, or run away from home or become teenage parents themselves. And the foundations of our community are weaker because of it.[3]*

Our prisons are filled with fatherless men and women—those with no father in the home at all or no father worth speaking of.

Two of my favorite faith-based movies are *The Shack* and *I Can Only Imagine*. Common themes in both include the damaging effect of an inadequate father; an abusive father; a father lost in his own pain who, in turn, inflicts pain on his family. Whether viewing this matter from a *necessary* spiritual perspective or simply through a sociological lens, the absence of fathers from the home or those present who lack a relationship with their Creator has created tremendous damage—just as Satan intended.

I have come to believe that many people transpose some, if not a great deal, of what they experienced with their father to their perception and understanding of God. This is a global, transcultural phenomenon. For this chapter I will only address this from the context of North America. I still quote from my journal *and . . .* I lived it!

What kind of father did you have—if you had one present in your life at all? Was he a workaholic and completely unavailable? Was he a busy man whom you didn't want to bother? Was he angry and emotionally distant? Was he toxically critical—someone you could never please? Was he abusive physically, sexually, emotionally, and/or psychologically? Did he treat your mother with love and respect or completely the opposite? Was there a lot of yelling and contention in your home—if you had a home? Do you recall him ever saying "I love you"? Was your father absent—a silent void in your life? Was he dead, in prison, addicted, unable to express his feelings, insufferably stubborn or simply gone . . . somewhere . . . other than where you were? Obviously, these many examples describe brokenness and deficiency.

On the other hand, was your father someone you admired and respected? Did he hug you and tell you often that you were loved? Did he take time to help you with your homework or explain the *why* of something with patience? Did you have father-son or father-daughter events and opportunities? Did he pray with you and talk with you about God? I will not list further positive traits and expressions of fatherhood for which you may have been the thankful recipient. The point is, we often approach God, hesitate to approach God, or outright reject God based on our family of origin and early childhood development. The presence or absence of a father in your life is most significant. The presence of a healthy, nurturing father is irreplaceably valuable.

I'd like to share a contemplative exercise I found useful when recalling the "dad" of my childhood, and my early impressions of

God. Go to your *comfortable* place alone, where there is little or no distraction; outside is best if you have a peaceful and favorite place to go. Ask God to open your heart and clear your mind. Take a notepad and pencil (which can be erased), or a tablet (which can be edited), to record your impressions. Try not to rush through this exercise in a few minutes, but rather give yourself a couple of hours. Now think about God the Father *and* your earthly father, almost as if toggling back and forth between two screens on your computer or between two photographs. Then record your thoughts. What did you discover?

What follows are two stories, with permission of the tellers, regarding the effects their fathers had on their life journeys. I will then share further thoughts in the next chapter on my own experience, both as a son and as a father.

Alton Hardy was born in the farming community of Sardis, about nine miles south of Selma, Alabama. He was the son of "Willie J," who had been a sharecropper since the age of five. Willie's parents had left him to fend for himself and he became a hardened survivor, knowing mostly his plow and his mule. Alton never had a bed off the floor. He slept on a thin mattress with two other siblings on the rough-hewn floorboards. "My father wasn't around much. When I was six, my mom and dad separated."

Alton grew up amongst the cotton fields in a "shotgun house" resting above ground on bricks. "I didn't know anything else existed. Since we had no transportation my mom would walk ten miles one way to the store in Selma, returning with six heavy bags of food," which didn't last long. But in this farming area, all of his now seven siblings could reduce their hunger by eating watermelon and other fruit and pecans from the trees when the landowners weren't looking. There was also a city dump behind their house. "For years it kept us alive. We could find some good stuff in there and sometimes discarded food." There was no electricity and one outhouse.

To break out of the confines of his limited existence, he said, "I'd walk as far as I could go out of town and then back again. Of course, I was barefoot, in tattered shorts, with no underwear and no t-shirt." Often this would take him over the Edmund Pettus Bridge crossing the Alabama River, named after the Confederate Army officer and grand dragon of the Ku Klux Klan. Completely unknown to Alton at the time was the historic importance of this site. In 1965, unarmed blacks marching peacefully for voting rights from Selma to Montgomery were attacked by Alabama police. This watershed event became known as "Bloody Sunday." In his youth Alton had a bad stutter and did not speak English well. He jokes about saying "hopper grass" instead of "grasshopper" and "dobbage bag" instead of "garbage bag." "Every day was meaningless. I had no hope. The worst poverty in Sardis was not the physical poverty, but living life without any dreams."

When Alton was twelve his oldest brother Eddie, who had completed military service and located work in Louisville, Kentucky, showed up one day with a U-Haul truck. They packed up their meager belongings, mom and seven siblings, and moved to a small Section 8 housing unit. When they first drove north on Interstate 65, Alton exclaimed how excited he was to see so many things he didn't know existed. He was amazed to use a phone, a toilet, and a shower for the first time. "I discovered a whole new world."

But that world also included direct racial prejudice. "In Selma, I didn't come into contact with whites much, because everything was segregated and it seemed normal. Sure, once in a while I would bale hay all day for a quarter, which seemed like a lot of money at the time. Then I would interact with whites, but mostly we lived in our own community. In Louisville I personally experienced regular racial prejudice." He recalls memories of riots and fighting in the schools. He started being called the N-word. One day walking home during his freshman year in high school, two white boys called him over to their car and both spat in his face. "It was the first of many times I experienced racial hostility." He explained, "Poverty was different in Louisville because we had to survive on one check from the government. In Sardis we could eat crops in the field. But here I experienced a lot of hungry nights."

Alton said his mother would cry a lot more here. She still walked miles to the store at the beginning of each month, but the food would run out about halfway through. He vividly recalls the regular visits from the social worker who would take a flashlight and search their unit to be sure that his father did not live there. "I didn't understand then how this was shaping my thinking. The federal government didn't want my father to be living with us to get our AFDC assistance. Here poverty really hit home. In Sardis we didn't have shoes and it didn't matter. In Louisville we didn't have shoes and we stood out. It was embarrassing."

He recalls his uncle and brother fighting over who should be responsible for caring for their family of eight and each agreed it was Willie J's responsibility. Then, they readily acknowledged that this was literally impossible. He was not capable of doing so.

For some reason—God's reason—Alton recalls being the only one of his siblings who regularly attended church. Near Sardis, his mother would take him to the East Salem Baptist Church. In Louisville she loved the Newburg Church of Christ and would wake him up to accompany her every week. He had to learn the sixty-six books of the Bible and basic knowledge of Christianity. "I knew of a God, but didn't yet fully understand the redemptive story of Jesus dying for me."

Alton also recalls an unexpected blessing at this church—ample amounts of glazed donuts and Oreo cookies. In the second half of each month this greatly helped to reduce his hunger. "It was at this church where I had a real encounter with the living Lord Jesus Christ. When I was baptized, I felt something was different in me." He describes listening intently to the preacher. "It was almost like God telling me one day you're going to do that." But since he still greatly stuttered, he wasn't sure if this was God's voice or just his wishful thinking.

Few of us realize at the time that the crucible experiences of our life—our struggles and doubts, the hard times—all will be used by God to shape us into the people he ordained us to become. I encourage you to listen to each of four riveting podcasts titled, "A Tree Grows in Selma—The Alton Hardy Story," produced by EPIC Media Partners.[4] Podcast #1 includes the story just described. Podcasts #2 and #3 tell of Alton's move north to live with his sister in Grand Rapids, Michigan. In these, he describes the completion of his high school years, playing college basketball, his determination to find work, and the struggle to keep his jobs in the face of even more sinister racial discrimination and outright hatred. He shares about his first marriage and eventual divorce and the uphill battle of taking the totality of his challenging life experiences and submitting them all to the will and purpose of his Creator.

Podcast #4 describes the transformative experience of Alton following God's direction, with his wife Sandra, to return to Birmingham, Alabama to establish Urban Hope. Choking back tears he proclaims forcefully, "The church didn't come to help my father or my family. But I say going forward we can't be divided no more. That's why I'm in urban ministry. We've got to be the unifying church. We can no longer be a church separated by pigmentation. That's what I'm saying . . . no more! That is what the enemy is trying to use against the church. God is raising up Christians to live a holistic Gospel that brings everyone to the foot of the cross. That's the heart of Alton Hardy."

One of my Starbucks buddies is Stan Dorn. He has a perpetually friendly smile on his face and always makes time to talk with people.

He usually wears a hat or t-shirt that includes some catchy phrase about Jesus, God, or the Bible. Stan is *never* shy to ask a person a direct question. I recall a particular lunch at a favorite Italian restaurant after he had finished a tile job at my house. I wanted to extend a small token of thanks, besides what I had agreed to pay him for his work. After the young server had taken our order, he asked her, "Do you ever go to church?" She responded, "No, not much anymore."

They continued a short exchange. When she brought the bread, oil, and balsamic he asked her, "Do you still read your Bible?" She responded, "Well, I used to, but no, I haven't in quite a while." After the food was delivered, he asked another question and then another. I thought to myself, *my goodness, I would never do this.* In fact, I sat at Starbucks for weeks with my nose buried in the paper, until Stan started to talk *with me.* And what a blessing it has been since.

Yet, right when he was getting to another question which would have started another series, I interrupted and asked the server, "Can I have some more marinara sauce, please?" I guess that's what you get when you mix "Bah humbug" with "It's a wonderful day in the neighborhood," at the same table!

The truth is, Stan has overcome some significant challenges to reach this place of openly sharing his faith in the Lord. He had a hard father, one who was distinctly hostile to the gospel. Stan said he never heard his father speak of God. He gave little direction to Stan, who had to find his way after many years of wandering. Income-wise Stan tried a range of things—lifeguard, boat worker, contractor, salesman, and various side jobs. At some point he *did* own a nice house, a boat, and more. But Stan was a ladies' man too, and went through three wives and quite a few more girlfriends. After coming to Christ, he expressed regret for how long it took him to actually obey him. Between his second and third wife Stan asked #2 to take their natural daughter back to live with her since #3 did not treat her well. This required his daughter to finish high school at a new school in another city, where she had no friends. Unfortunately, wife #2 had a new man in the house. The full story is still not told openly. His daughter's trauma was marinated in anger then atrophied into rage.

Just two years ago, unable to live on his meager social security check, with no pension or investments, Stan asked to move into his now-married daughter's house with a husband and two kids. Stan enjoyed his preschool-aged granddaughters. But morning after morning during our coffee time, I listened to the devastating tales of a clearly wounded daughter lashing out at him. Everything was his fault. And most often it was communicated with acidic anger at a high decibel level. Stan's life had changed and now radiated God's love. He did so much around their house. Built things. Bought things. Tried to encourage. He spoke to his granddaughters about God, but was harshly reprimanded by his daughter for doing so. She blasphemed the Lord, calling him "the spaghetti monster in the sky." After a year of listening to the criticism, disrespect, and outright abuse, I helped Stan relocate to Prescott, Arizona, where he has now peacefully started a new life.

A father's role in the well-being of his children is critical. Satan knows exactly where to strike. God, our Father, is able to redeem our failures, but it will take time, and happen according to his will and purpose. One of the most debilitating experiences we all feel, to some extent or a large extent, is not having been the perfect father or mother. If *only* we could do it over again. We can't. The fantastic reality is that it's never too late to start. As long as we have breath, God can and will redeem what has been broken.

Chapter 6
BEING A FATHER

Imagine who you want your kids to become. Be that.
— *Anonymous*

*I*n chapter 1 you learned a bit about my family and formative years. Let me add a few more insights. My natural mother, Louise, experienced evident trauma in her early life, including an alcoholic father who would physically push her away. He did not love her. She was forced to attend a parochial high school she greatly resented. In her senior year she was misdiagnosed by a nun/nurse who claimed, mistakenly, that she would only live a few years more. As a result, mom was denied access to the nursing program she had set her heart on. This crushed mom's dreams, and she moved into her twenties with a sense of disorientation.

Until her death at age ninety-two, mom spewed her misguided loathing on the Catholic church, blaming the Pope for nearly every economic, social, and personal ill. Sadly, when her sister Edna died, Louise refused to attend her funeral because mom swore that she would never set foot in a Roman Catholic church again.

When mom became impregnated by a man she apparently met casually, she blamed him for most everything else that wasn't covered in her evident misandry and psychological transference. After I was born, and his departure, she locked down all access to information about my birth father in every respect. *Her view* was she was protecting me, but in fact, she was hiding her pain. During one conversation in my fifties she responded to my request, for the umpteenth time, to tell me his medical history. She proclaimed, incredulously, "You don't have any of his genes. You have 100 percent of *my* genes." These various traumas in mom's life distinctly affected her understanding of a loving and forgiving God. The unsuccessful search, the void, from my never knowing my birth father also contributed to my formative understanding of my Heavenly Father. Over time, God himself transformed my understanding of his love for me.

At four years old, while playing in a park one Sunday afternoon, I ran up to a nice man sitting on a park bench and became the matchmaker. Chauncey and Louise were married, and I was adopted by age five. My observation of the fathers and home life of closer friends created the realization that there was a certain dysfunction in our family dynamic. I was too young to fully understand what that was. Dad was kind, somewhat plodding, but a faithful and committed man. With a pierced eardrum from his youth he didn't hear very well or communicate effectively. Despite this and other limitations he trusted God and did his best. Dad poured himself into scouting and invested his time to teach me invaluable life skills.

We had very little financial resources, yet Dad had a heart for the disadvantaged. He committed us to driving two hours round trip each Sunday to a state-run institution to pick up two simply dressed but decidedly eager developmentally delayed adolescents. They *so* appreciated the chance to get out of their restricted environment and join our family to attend church and share a meal at a local restaurant. Dad nursed birds with a broken wing and helped them return to their habitat. As I grew more mature in my Christian faith, I realized my criticisms of him were both petty and misplaced. As we already observed from Scripture, it clearly indicates that God uses the weak and the simple to accomplish His purposes. Ultimately, my life could have been *much worse*. God gave me a father when I could have had none. Decades later (4/22/19), I wrote this journal entry:

> *Thank you, Lord, for Chauncey. He taught me how to tie my Boy Scout knots, how to light a campfire, how to honor and preserve your creation. And he modeled how to live with a contentious wife and love her with all her flaws. He taught me how to know you, Lord, and how to pray. Yet he taught me little about financial management or how to fix a car or participate in sports. He couldn't help me with my homework or teach me the manly trades. He didn't show me how to fish, play golf, or sail a boat. But he was your instrument, Holy Father, and he saved me from being fatherless. He mowed half the lawn and painted half of our little house, which I finished. He never remembered mom's birthday or their anniversary. I paid for his plane tickets to visit us when we moved across country, and I worked hard to pay for my own education. But he modeled how to honor you Lord and he prayed for me. I could have been an orphan and homeless or unwanted—left with a needy and neurotic mother. But he showed me enough to make me determined and persevering, to strike out on my own, alone but sufficiently able! He left me not a penny, but instead a heart of gold.*

Being a father was a joy and one of the supreme highlights of my life. In succession, over a four-year period, I was blessed with three wonderful daughters. Of course, there are always challenges, but I loved each of them with all my heart. I did my very best to be a great dad. My firstborn, Bristol Michelle, arrived on my birthday, April 7. By age two she was diagnosed with a debilitating neurological condition. Her medical care over an eight-year period, until she died at age ten, created challenge and complexity in our family. Her acute medical needs added great stress in our family and in relationship with my wife. Our marriage ended in divorce. Many couples with terminally ill children do divorce, though this was not the primary reason.

Bristol, two years old   *Bristol grave site*

When Bristol died, we asked persons attending her memorial service to make a donation instead of food or flowers. We collectively sent this love gift to Focus on the Family, still led at that time by Dr. James Dobson. His response was so comforting and genuine. He later included the letter I wrote in his book *When God Doesn't Make Sense*, as well as his December year-end communique.

Sometime later our pastor planned to present a series of videos of real-life stories for a sermon series. My testimony of God's faithfulness in the midst of such a heavy burden was later posted on You Tube. The title (selected by the producer) is "Ralph's Story," but it most certainly is "Bristol's Story."[1] She was a true gift, "Our little angel from the Lord"—which is exactly what is inscribed on her gravestone.

I had a pounding headache and a bone-weariness after that first full day of calling family and friends to let them know our Bristol had died. I also had a myriad of initial arrangements to make. *Each* of us experience this when a family member passes into eternity. It was necessary to put my grief aside for a while, to attend to what needed to be done. That first night, I wanted to tell my sweet girl that I missed her, so I sat at my desk to pour out my soul. This is the letter that flowed out, without one word of editing or correction.

—◆—│—◆—

My Dear Bristol,

Before you were born, I prayed for you. In my heart I knew that you would be a little angel. And, so you were!

When you were born on my birthday, April 7, it was evident that you were a special gift from the Lord. But how profound a gift you turned out to be. More than the beautiful bundle of gurgles and rosy cheeks . . . more than the first born of my flesh, a joy unspeakable . . . you showed me God's love more than anything else in creation. Bristol, you taught me how to love.

I certainly loved you when you were cuddly and cute, when you rolled over and sat up and jabbered your first words. I loved you when the searing pain of realization took hold that something was wrong . . . that you were not developing as quickly as your peers. And then when we understood it was more serious than that. I loved you when we went from hospital to clinic to doctor looking for a medical diagnosis that would bring some hope. And, of course, we always prayed for you . . . and prayed . . . and prayed. I loved you when one of the tests resulted in too much spinal fluid being drawn from your body and you screamed. I loved you when you moaned and cried, when your mom and I and your sisters would drive for hours late at night to help you fall asleep. I loved you with tears in my eyes when, confused, you would bite your fingers or your lip by accident, and when your eyes crossed and then went blind.

I most certainly loved you when you could no longer speak, but how profoundly I missed your voice! I loved you when your scoliosis started wrenching your body like a pretzel, when we put a tube in your stomach so you could eat because you were choking on your food, which we fed you one spoonful at a time for up to two hours per meal. I managed to love you when your contorted limbs would not allow ease of changing your messy diapers . . . so many diapers . . . ten years of diapers. Bristol, I even loved you when you could not say the one thing I longed to hear back, "Daddy, I love you." Bristol, I loved you when I was close to God and when he seemed far away, when I was full of faith and also when I was angry at him.

And the reason I loved you, my Bristol, in spite of these difficulties, is that God put this love in my heart. This is the wonderous nature of God's love, that he loves us even when we are blind or deaf or twisted . . . in body or in spirit. God loves us even when we can't tell him that we love him back.

My dear Bristol, now you are free! I look forward to that day, according to God's promises, when we will be joined together with you with the Lord, completely whole and full of joy. I'm so happy that you have your crown first. We will follow you someday . . . in his time.

Before you were born, I prayed for you. In my heart I knew that you would be a little angel. And, so you were!

Love,
Daddy

———◆—┃—◆———

Chelsea Joy is my middle daughter. Vibrant, sensitive, and determined, she was our Miss Michigan pageant contestant (in the Miss America track) and later a certified WBFF (World Beauty, Fitness & Fashion) "pro." A graduate of Azusa Pacific University, she now operates her own social media company and is married to Mario, her *guapo* Argentinian soccer player.

Misty Nicole is my smart, conscientious, hard charger. A two-time NAIA national champion soccer player at Westmont College, she is a Human Resources professional and married to "football buff" Dusty, who works at NASA's Jet Propulsion Laboratory (JPL) in Pasadena.

There is little point in *my* telling you what kind of father I was. What follows is my favorite birthday gift of *all time*, on my sixtieth, from Chelsea and Misty (with Bristol already in heaven). It is framed and displayed in my office, with humility and thanks to our Heavenly Father for his mercy and answer to my prayer.

Chelsea and Misty

60 Things We Love about You, Dad

1. You are a loving father.

2. You persevere through all things.

3. Your tenacity and determination in all that you do.

4. You taught us how to ride our first bike.

5. How you are able to forgive.

6. Your wisdom and thoughtful advice.

7. The way you constantly encourage us.

8. Your sincerity and authenticity.

9. How you portray God's love.

10. The way you face challenges head-on.

11. How smart and intelligent you are.

12. Your gift of helping others.

13. How you can be thoughtful and reflective.

14. Your passion for traveling the world.

15. When you blink your eyes really fast when you laugh.

16. The way you fold your toes together (ha ha).

17. Your ability to be a great provider.

18. That you bought each of us our first car—what a great memory!

19. The dimple in your chin.

20. You supported us by coming to all of our soccer games and sporting events.

21. You always worked hard to give us the best.

22. You showed us what it means to never give up.

23. Your kind spirit and generous heart.

24. Your international experiences—and our trip to Africa!

25. Your early and ambitious work hours.

26. The way you are always willing to provide a listening ear.

27. Your organizational skills.

28. That you went above and beyond your fatherly duties to raise your little angel, Bristol.

29. The confidence you have in yourself.

30. That we get to laugh together with you.

31. How you always encourage us to dream big.

32. When you chased burglars down the street in your underwear and Birkenstocks.

33. How you are optimistic in the face of adversity.

34. The way you are willing to sacrifice and put others before yourself.

35. The gap in your teeth.

36. That you are "hyper boy" at times.

37. The way you always believe in us.

38. How you can get a tan, just like that.

39. Your laugh and smile.

40. How you taught us that we can do anything we put our minds to.

41. Your ability to be a strategic business planner, developer, and entrepreneur.

42. How you always unbuckle your seatbelt before getting to the driveway.

43. That you taught us the importance of education and put us through college.

44. That you are slow to anger and patient with us when we make mistakes.

45. How you empower and motivate us.

46. The way you carefully nurture us as your daughters.

47. That you give us good advice on life based on your wisdom and experience.

48. You recognize each of our individual strengths.

49. How you always make it a priority to take our phone call.

50. The way you love jazz music so much.

51. How you say "yestaday" and "quater" from your East Coast upbringing.

52. The way you can add up numbers in your head without counting on your fingers!

53. Your adventurous spirit in constant search of new journeys.

54. That you are like a fine wine, getting better with age :-)

55. The way you supported us growing up.

56. How you encourage us to be prayerful in all things.

57. The way you always remind us that you love us.

58. That you are not just our father but also our friend.

59. How you love us unconditionally.

60. Knowing that you are always there for us no matter what.

Love always,
Chelsea & Misty

I cannot offer any better summary of the importance and impact of a father—as seen through the eyes of his children. And I cannot tell you with any more passion and urgency, that God loves you more than you will ever know, regardless of what kind of father you had. *All* he has asked us, fathers *and* mothers, to do . . . is to love one another! If you didn't do it before, it's never too late to start.

I conclude with this father's prayer from John Eldredge—for every father who wants to be as much like our Father as possible to our children and family:

Father—from whom all fatherhood derives its name—
I pray that from your glorious, unlimited resources you
would give me
a mighty inner strength by the power of your Spirit in my
inner being.
I pray that Jesus Christ will be more and more at home in
my heart;
I pray that my roots would go down deep into the soil of
your marvelous love –
that I would be rooted and grounded in love, that I would
have the power
to understand how wide, long, high and how deep your love
really is.
I pray to know, really know and experience, the love of
Christ,
so that I will be filled with the fullness of life and power
that comes from above.[2]

Chapter 7

FREEDOM IS NOT FREE

If I'm free, it's because I'm always running.
— Jimi Hendrix

The above quote represents a popular philosophy of freedom. It was boldly expressed by American psychedelic rock guitarist James Marshall "Jimi" Hendrix, arguably one of the most influential of his generation. He died in Nottingham, London, UK at the age of twenty-eight from asphyxia caused by barbiturate intoxication complicated by chronic fatigue and sleep deprivation. In plain English, he choked on his vomit from an overdose of drugs while exhausted. Jimi also reportedly struggled with a range of relationship insecurities, as well as disillusionment with the music industry and with life itself.

My intention here is not to describe a formal classification of disorder. Rather, I am painting a few broad brushstrokes on the canvas. This brand of living presupposes that *freedom* is experienced when you control your own life, go your own way, do your own thing, and follow what makes you happy, for as long as you are able to do so. If we stop running, then something bad will catch up to us and we will ostensibly lose our freedom.

It is rather cliché, as well as condescending, to consider most rockers as hard-living consumers of sex, drugs, and alcohol, though many were. Change a few props in the production and a few details in the script and I would suggest that many of us—the majority of us—have followed a similar path in our desire to be "free." We run hard and pursue *our* goals. I know I did. My story—and perhaps yours—is likely packaged in a respectable career, mostly stable relationships, wholesome hobbies, memorable vacations, and sufficient church involvement. However, the basis upon which we define "freedom" and embrace it requires further consideration. What we perceive and pursue as freedom, for many, is the biggest stumbling block to understanding what God desires in our relationship with him, and the true freedom we can experience.

Love, by necessity, involves freedom of choice. Therefore, love *always* involves risk. In a healthy binary relationship two persons must be free to love the other, with the understanding that one may not do so with the same intensity, in the same manner, or with the same commitment as the other. Both must have the power to think and act without hindrance or restraint. Scripture and society each put guideposts in place, with traditions and expectations to follow, but individual freedom of choice is the ultimate determinant. It is the fortunate couple that discovers the equilibrium and contentment that comes out of this mutually engaged freedom. It seems easier to grasp this concept when considering human relationships. It is a bit trickier when we apply these variables to our relationship with God. If we diligently study God's Word, we will discover that the framework is very much the same.

At the apex of God speaking forth the earth into existence, his crowning event was the creation of humankind: "Then God said, let us make mankind in our image, in our likeness, so that they may rule . . . So God created mankind in his own image, in the image of God he created them, male and female he created them" (Gen. 1:26–27). And the heavenly hosts marveled when he did so. God, too, wanted a loving relationship with his creation—and this can only exist by mutual choice. God already decided to love us. He gave us free will, to reciprocate with our love. He first loved us and desires the same in return.

One of the great confessions of the Christian faith says, "Man's chief end is to glorify God, and to enjoy him forever."[1] Plainly stated, this is the eternal reason for our existence. We are allotted an amount of time while on earth, in this temporal body, to seek God and believe in him. Those who desire to do so *will* find God and *will* remain with him for eternity. Those with the freedom given to them, who prefer not to do so, *will not* continue to exist in God's presence for eternity. It's really that simple. Throw in the words "sin" and "hell" and many people reject these truths, but they shouldn't. Pursuing our eternal freedom is our own choice. Now let's consider the alternative.

My life's work involved many memorable trips to Vietnam. During the war, the US Selective Service held lotteries drafting young men for military service. My lottery number was below the induction threshold, unlike a lot of guys in my high school senior class. (As I already shared, I volunteered to serve in the Navy some years later, after securing my bachelor's and master's degrees.) The immediate years following the withdrawal of US forces were filled with pain and dislocation for the people of southern Vietnam starting at the demilitarized zone, a 150-mile-long cease fire line on the 38th parallel. The iconoclastic withdrawal of the final evacuees in US helicopters from the rooftop of the US Embassy in Saigon on March 29, 1973 will remain a stain on the legacy of the political leaders who mismanaged this war.

My first engagement in Vietnam was October 1988 following President Reagan's selection of General John Vessey (the tenth chairman of the Joint Chiefs of Staff). He was given the specific assignment of special envoy to Vietnam to address the status of those missing in action (MIAs). With a useful skill in networking and procurement, I was the only American on a special four-person team—with my

Filipino friend Milton Amayun, MD, MPH and two Australians—to travel to Hanoi. Our task was to identify and develop one of the first post-war humanitarian initiatives. In these days, Vietnam was an economic and political mess. Between 1975 and 1997 more than 1.6 million Vietnamese had fled for America, Canada, Australia, and other nations. There were 900,000 that processed through the cumbersome and time-consuming Orderly Departure Program. But 700,000, who were under threat of reeducation camps or death, became part of a steady stream of tragic, nighttime flotillas of "boat people." In later interviews, we learned that two thousand or more individuals and families would depart in makeshift boats every month with 40 percent ending in tragic death, usually by drowning. Others were preyed upon, robbed, raped, or killed by pirates who intentionally tracked them.

Our visas and transit approval were processed through Bangkok, Thailand. Upon arrival we debriefed with UNICEF and UNDP staff on our proposed itinerary. They were most helpful in giving us perspective on the circumstances we would face. Flying into the tropical green surrounding Hanoi, I saw what appeared to be many fishponds inside miles of rice paddy fields. The bright sun glistened off the calm water. These were, in fact, bomb craters never leveled or filled in. Dotting the landscape were women wearing their traditional *nón lá*, bamboo palm leaf conical hats. Arriving at Noi Bai Airport and after much bureaucratic red tape, our passports were stamped and we were met by representatives of "The People's Committee." They drove us to our hotel by car through streets teeming with bicycles and people tending small cooking fires on the side of the road.

Our transportation the remainder of this visit was by human-powered three-wheel "cyclos." Later, as we passed children, they would shout "din-so, din-so." We learned this meant "Russian." During this postwar period most aid, military support, and commercial activity came from the Soviet Union (before The Supreme Soviet voted itself out of existence on December 26, 1991). The Russians essentially took over all former American bases and assets in the country. We had an intense and critically important schedule to get through, just two days before Prince Sihanouk of Cambodia and General Vessey were to arrive.

From my perspective, communist countries depend on aggressive internal and external propaganda. If you're patient, you can get past it. When common human needs and aspirations surface, bonding is attainable with the people you are working with. Our itinerary started with obligatory government appointments—Ministry of Health; Ministry of Labour, Invalids, and Social Affairs; Ministry of Foreign Affairs; and AIDRECEP, the coordinating body for all western humanitarian assistance. We were asked to focus on the need for prosthetics and orthotics—considering the multiple thousands of civilians who lost limbs, some from the war, many more from unexploded ordinance which continued to be set off by innocent civilians for years following.

We were also "offered" the opportunity to visit some historic sights. This included the diminutive statue at Trúc Bạch Lake where John McCain's A-4E Skyhawk jet was shot down, as well as the creepy prison compound dubbed "the Hanoi Hilton" by the POWs imprisoned and tortured there. McCain was held here for six years. We were taken to the Vietnam Military History Museum opposite Lenin Park and the Ho Chi Minh Mausoleum, where "Chairman Ho" was encased in a refrigerated glass coffin. This was located on—what else, Điện Biên Phủ Boulevard, site of the Viet Minh victory over the French. Here piles of destroyed US military equipment were overshadowed by the Flag Tower flying a humongous flag of The Socialist Republic of Vietnam. Inside the actual museum building were numerous photos of POWs in compromised positions, anti-war demonstrators in US streets, Lyndon Johnson with his head in his hands, and, of course, a few smiling shots of "Hanoi Jane" Fonda. I believe you are getting the picture of what I meant by aggressive propaganda.

Oliver North at John McCain statue, Hanoi   *Military Museum Hanoi*

So, how does one "get past" all of this? Chapter 13, "Forgiveness and Healing," takes a stab at this challenge. Here I will say that we had the option to respond either in a political manner or from a kingdom perspective. The choice is both clear and profound, but by no means easy.

We flew south to Quang Nam Da Nang province and visited what became the focal point of our initial project assistance, The Da Nang Orthopedic and Rehabilitation Hospital. The patients were *supremely* patient—waiting for the long-shot chance of receiving a custom-made limb and individualized therapy. The people ranged from young children to the aged, each with a sad story to tell. The staff was warm, genuine, and engaging. It was mutually felt by our delegation, the staff, and the officials in Hanoi that this location and area of specialized humanitarian assistance was the most needed and the best fit. When I returned to the States, I was the key facilitator in a major initiative between the US Veterans Administration and private prosthetics companies to provide prefabricated limbs. More importantly I secured the raw materials—the resins, mesh, cast forms, tools, and training to create patient-appropriate prostheses and help build a new life for those injured.

Our visit included the Hoi An Orphanage, the underground hospital at Marble Mountain, and lunch and a swim at beautiful China Beach where US servicemen spent much of their R&R time. And similar to the war era, we were occasionally approached by "coffee girls" who would invite themselves to our table for coffee while *trying* to negotiate services beyond the culinary.

Street scene Da Nang

Our final stop was Saigon. Each location we visited began with a required exchange with The People's Committee to approve our itinerary and assign a *minder*, someone who accompanied us throughout our schedule. We toured and then offered advice or some assistance to Bach Mai Hospital, Ho Chi Minh Rehabilitation Center, and various communal poly clinics, each significantly short of vital supplies. Russian MiGs intermittently flew overhead, some breaking the sound barrier.

We made a memorable side trip to the Cu Chi Tunnels, an immense network of underground tunnels, five stories deep, hand-dug by the Viet Cong. They housed the stealth fighters involved in the 1968 Tet Offensive and other campaigns that brought sleepless nights and indiscriminate terror to the GIs on guard duty. As many as sixteen thousand men and women were cramped into these claustrophobic, interconnected spaces infested with ants, venomous centipedes, snakes, scorpions, spiders, and rodents. Viet Cong fighters and sympathizers would spend their day underground, working to expand this tunnel network, then come out at night to scavenge food, tend their crops, and engage US troops in guerilla-tactic skirmishes. Cu Chi was a poignant reminder of the grit and determination of the Vietnamese people.

In the dozen years that followed I likely traveled to Vietnam at least twenty times. We expanded our recipient partners to include numerous hospitals, clinics, and orphanages, moving beyond prosthetics to support of primary health care and some specialized medical services such as cancer treatment. I became very fond of the Vietnamese people, and they reciprocated with kindness. Eventually, after becoming CEO of another charity, I established cultural exchange/work tours for many former US veterans. We established a dual purpose for these trips. To the extent possible we exposed them to opportunities for emotional healing, and we facilitated tangible connections for human compassion to people who greatly appreciated it. We always provided some opportunity to see the beauty of the country. This included the picturesque drive north on Highway 1 over the Hải Vân Pass toward Hue, Halong Bay, My Son, My Khe Beach (China Beach), Hang Son Doong Cave, and Nha Trang. If you ever consider traveling to Vietnam, I highly encourage you to do so. It's a beautiful country to explore.

Our most "famous" visitor on one subsequent trip was Oliver North, whom we hosted with a writer and videographer. This resulted in the publishing of his second book, *One More Mission: Oliver North Returns to Vietnam*. Our mission was to get him as close as possible to the site where he actually served in combat. With planning and permission, we went north on Highway 1 from Da Nang into Quang Tri Province. Then at a designated latitude, we made a left turn west into the mountains then finally turned north on dirt road until we reached Hill 9 where young North served his country from 1968–1969. He writes of two landmasses he saw again, the Rockpile and the Razorback, where battlefield bloodshed is etched in his memory.

Vietnam is not a pleasant recollection for many American GIs. Three million of America's sons and 11,500 of its daughters served in this war and nearly sixty thousand died in combat. Even worse and shameful was their treatment upon returning home to a politically divided America. For "Ollie" and most of the servicemen that came with us in subsequent years, they were in full agreement. "Yet in spite of all this, from the northern tip of the country, south all the way to what is now Ho Chi Minh City, there is no evidence of hostility or animosity toward Americans, 'We want you to come back' was the cry we heard most from the people. More than once we were told, 'We love Americans.' In fact, the only danger that Americans face in Vietnam is to be mistakenly identified as Russians. The Vietnamese very clearly don't like the Russians."[2]

Freedom—isn't free. To live in peace, with opportunity, requires sacrifice. Freedom in Christ *is* a free gift to us, but it too required a supreme sacrifice. The flip side of freedom is not just restriction or inconvenience. Ultimately, it is *bondage*. The path to bondage is a journey of incremental entrapment and deception. And there is an enemy who is highly skilled at this.

Chapter 8
THE FROG IN THE KETTLE

Love has wings, not anchors. — **T. F. Hodge**

The Philippines and its friendly people bring a smile to my face often. I have traveled here dozens of times. Over the years I supported the health and community development work of my dear friend Rufino "Rufi" Macagba, MD, MPH. He leads the highly acclaimed Lorma Medical Center and Lorma Schools[1] in San Fernando, La Union, northern Luzon. Ranked as a center of excellence, LMC is the leading private Category 3 hospital in Region 1. When I secured a US State Department grant to provide bio-medical safety and laboratory equipment training in collaboration with the Ministry of Health in Uganda, East Africa, I recruited the highly qualified Lorma biotechs. And as a board member of the Lorma Community Development Foundation, I support their goal of planting millions of cashew and cacao plants to add economic opportunity to the region.

I encourage you to visit this part of the Philippines. And en route, you can enjoy the white sandy beaches along their west coast or the cool mountain tourist region of Baguio, previously the site of a US military base, Camp John Hay.

South of greater metro Manila, in *Dasmariñas, Cavite,* where my medical products LLC has a small sales office. It is operated by my *kumpadre* "Jun," who receives regular moral support from his wife, my *kumare, Doctora* KC. I am also the *ninong* (godfather) to their son Jacob. Individually or together we have done business in multiple provinces in Luzon and Visayas, as far south as Davao City in Mindanao with inroads into General Santos City, home of renowned boxer Manny Pacquiao. When possible, I would also find time for a restful getaway excursion to some of the beautiful beaches of Palawan and their offshore islands. Over the years I have made friends with many Filipinos and have, by extension of these relationships, met hundreds of men and women of all ages and stages of life. Through business, church, and social settings, I have learned much about their culture.

One of the universal tendencies of Filipinos is their willingness to sacrifice personal need and comfort to support their family. Filipinos who live and work as expatriates or Overseas Filipino Workers, as they are official designated, are found throughout the world in a multitude of fields. There are many well-educated, articulate Filipinos in medical and allied health, hospitality and cruise industry, engineers, military-support specialists, and more. There are also a great number of lesser skilled and less educated Filipinos who secure contract employment in caregiving, domestic services, and multiple industries requiring manual labor. They come from the thousands of poor *barangays* in districts and regions far flung throughout the two thousand inhabited islands out of a total 7,641 islands which make up The Philippines.

One of my friends, who is a pastor and church planter in a remote region of Mindanao, has an unmarried daughter with two kids, helping with the greater family finances as a housekeeper and nanny in Doha, Qatar. I try to encourage her by sending an occasional chat message or worship song on YouTube. Her employers are strict Muslims who do not allow her any freedom. This is one of her Messenger chats: "They don't treat me well. I feel empty inside. All I want is for them to give me time to go to church, but they won't. I can't even sing praises to God or say the name of Jesus. It makes me cry. We work seven days a week and I am so tired. I am forever thankful for your prayers. Thank you so much Ralph. I receive it right now in Jesus's name." Together, the combined income of this family is very modest and barely covers their needs. This weight presses in on everyone and explains their willingness to sacrifice at all cost.

I described this one family unit to make a larger point about another track of income generation. It is my observation that a very insidious slope toward bondage occurs in barely perceptible, incremental stages. To divide the labor among many hands, families in poverty often have multiple children. Education is limited and inadequate when available. Income is seasonal and sporadic. Discouragement is endemic and often leads to desperate choices. Many young women have children out of wedlock, with the inseminator nowhere to be found—I decline to use the word "father." Despair forces the young to migrate to larger metropolitan areas. Young men take on labor, driver, security, and other jobs which require little training. Young women take on food service, sales, housekeeping, and other jobs. Some of the pretty ones, *too many*, discover that they can earn many times more income working in the commercial sex industry. There are various forms including massage parlors, karaoke clubs, and directly in prostitution offering "in *or* out call" services. Many have one or two kids left with the *barangay* parent(s) and take on the economic responsibility of the entire extended family. Each has a story of misfortune and financial stress which adds to the complexity and desperation of their eventual decisions. This is not just theory. I have known some in this precise situation.

Of course, the slope toward bondage is gradual, like the proverbial frog in the heating kettle. Many young ladies hire on as hostesses just to sit and drink with the guy. "Umbrella girls" accompany their golf partners to shield them from sun or rain. But the real money is in full service. By the time a girl gets to this stage the trap has been set. Regular fund transfers back home are now needed and expected.

Moral inhabitations initially set aside "for a while" have long since been eliminated. Some end up in seedy places like P. Burgos Street in Makati, Metro Manila, or Angeles City 84 kilometers north on the E1 or E4. The clubs here attract a particular type of international clientele.

Women who continue in this trade soon realize there is greater economic opportunity in places like Singapore or Tokyo. Too many stories are told of the Filipina who accepted a contract in Japan for a club gig, only to find that she was now *owned* and abused by the Yakuza crime syndicate, forced into excessive and repetitive service in a brothel. If she comes out alive, she's lucky.

Singapore's Geylang District is no different, only the business is run by the Chinese. When the young Filipina arrives having signed a contract, she learns that besides the "loan" she took for the airfare, visa, and in-processing, there is also rent for her bed in a dormitory setting with other girls plus other expenses they must pay out of their promised salary. Passports are taken for safekeeping and put in a locked file. Quickly the nervous young lady discovers, to her shock, that she doesn't make enough just bar hosting. You can see the inevitable trap they are in. I've actually paid off the contracts of a few of these girls, who were friends of friends of mine, to get them out of their situation.

The more cautious girls stay near home and ply their trade on one of the online sites. But the results are the same—a constricting path of fewer options, unexpected dependence, toxic shame, and hopelessness. It becomes a bondage that devours all but the fortunate ones. And I haven't even touched on the epicenter of sexual deviance and sex tourism: Thailand. Here places like Patpong, Cowboy Soi, Phukhet, and Pattaya attract men from around the globe. Actually, the sex trade persists throughout much of Asia, and this type of exploitation and bondage exists on every continent!

Let me briefly address a different type of bondage which occurs all over the world—human trafficking. It is an evil which happens in plain sight, in many of our communities. The three most prevalent categories are forced labor, domestic servitude, and sexual enslavement. The third is particularly prevalent in the US. In America there is still no *legal* access to onsite commercial sex, but opportunities exist in the shadows. Sex trafficking in the US is an ominous cancer. As I was driving recently, the radio news announced a new training program to sensitize first responders and the general public to learn about the signs of trafficking and behaviors to look for. Research indicates the revenue from sex trafficking is the second-largest in the underground economy after drug trafficking, in the hundreds of millions. If you research this topic you will get victim statistics that run the gamut, up to as many as 68,000 per day! Girls as young as ten through late teens, some even older, are either "groomed" or outright kidnapped.

Professionals who work with these victims have described at least three techniques, often in combination, used to lure or scare young girls into prostitution.[2] The "Romeo pimp" showers attention and gifts on the girl and gets her to fall in love with him. He becomes her boyfriend—until he turns on her. The "CEO pimp" offers a job, an enticing amount of money, or a new opportunity, usually requiring the girl to change locations. The "job" waiting is not what was promised. And there is the "Gorilla pimp." From the start, he is violent and abusive. Often the girl is drugged or beaten and is told that if she ever talks, her family will be harmed or killed. Imagine being a frightened young lady and finding yourself in this horrific situation. Imagine your daughter or granddaughter disappearing into this nightmare.

There are, of course, many other varieties of bondage. Some may start out as "fun," then turn into a habit, which morphs into an addiction. Drugs, alcohol, inhalants, prescriptions, other substance abuse, gambling, and gluttony start this way. Other compulsive behaviors include stealing, excessive work, starting fires, self-cutting, inducing pain, and spiritual obsession (as opposed to religious devotion).[3] There is also a global system of economic entrapment where low-skilled and poorly educated workers are forced to work in sweatshops with suffocating hours and unacceptable conditions. Inhumane labor practices and child labor exist in many countries, some even hidden in plain sight in western countries. Lastly, there is the hidden forced labor inside China's vast prison labor system producing goods for many global brands. These multinational companies look the other way or claim not to benefit from such practices, but they are complicit. Injustice and, therefore, bondage are rampant in each of these categories in virtually every corner of the planet. It is a travesty.

As an astute reader you will realize that I have utilized different terms without defining them—addiction, mental disorders, bondage. There is formal, scientific, and voluminous information available on each of these. Here, let me simply offer a general definition of bondage: "servitude, serfdom, subjection, enslavement, subjugation, oppression, restraint, imprisonment."[4] It is important for Christ-followers, those spiritually discerning, to fully recognize both the source of freedom and the origin of bondage. The next chapter, "The Enemy Is the Enemy," will focus on the originating evil behind many addictions, mental disorders, and other forms of bondage. Faith and reason, science and mysticism . . . some believe you can only embrace one *or* the other. I do not.

A humanistic, secular perspective will ascribe the origin of most, if not all, types of bondage to human behavioral and psychological variables. For those who understand that God created humans with a body, a psyche, and a spirit, this perspective changes. "Though the influence of Enlightenment rationalism has been quite effective in causing many . . . to deny the existence of Satan and demons, or at least to minimize their activity . . . it is not, as some claim, simply an outmoded primitive worldview that holds that demons exist. Nor is Jesus simply a good psychologist. Both the New Testament and ministry experience show that demons, unlike psychological problems, are separate beings that live in people, can talk and can be eliminated through the authoritative use of the power of Jesus Christ."[5] Clearly, this topic elicits multiple points of view. I am communicating my position from my understanding of Scripture.

I have embraced, by faith believing and by comprehending knowledge, that our choice is not either/or, but rather, both/and. At some time in our life, we must choose between light or darkness, between freedom or bondage. Yet, we are incapable of finding the light or living in true freedom without a mediator.

Is there a way out? I don't think there is—at least not on my side. It often seems that the more I try to disentangle myself from the darkness, the darker it becomes. I need light, but that light has to conquer my darkness and that I cannot bring about myself. I cannot forgive myself. I cannot make myself feel loved. By myself I cannot leave the land of my anger. I cannot bring myself home nor can I create communion on my own. I can desire it, hope for it, wait for it, yes pray for it. But my true freedom I cannot fabricate for myself. That must be given to me. I am lost. I must be found and brought home by the shepherd who goes out to me. The story of the prodigal son is the story of a God who goes searching for me and who doesn't rest until he has found me. He urges and he pleads. He begs me to stop clinging to the powers of death and to let myself be embraced by arms that will carry me to the place where I will find the life I most desire.[6]

So, if the Son sets you free, you will be free indeed.
(John 8:36)

Chapter 9
THE ENEMY IS THE ENEMY

Be alert and of sober mind. Your enemy the devil
prowls around like a roaring lion looking for
*someone to devour. — **1 Peter 5:8***

A terrorist uses deception, intimidation, and violence in pursuit of a political objective. The most effective terrorist is a hidden one. He strikes at his victim's most vulnerable point of access, while he is unaware and unguarded.

Over the past decade, terrorists have killed an average of 21,000 people per year.[1] Terrorists often work in groups. Most are hidden. A sleeper cell refers to "a secretive group of spies or terrorists that remain inactive within a target population until ordered to act." Our news has been saturated with increasing incidents of terror perpetrated in many forms on the citizens of many countries.

Lest we forget, what follows are just some of the thousands of increasing attacks around the world which have taken place over these recent decades: Twin Towers—9-11; bombing of the US Embassy in Beirut; TWA Flight 847; US housing complex at Khobar Towers, Saudi Arabia; bombings of US embassies in Nairobi, Kenya, and Dar es Salaam, Tanzania; attack on Israeli embassy in Buenos Aires, Argentina; Benghazi attacks on two US compounds in Libya; attack on West Berlin discotheque; Pan Am Flight 73; King David Hotel, Jerusalem;

simultaneous massacres in a Paris stadium, restaurants, and later the newspaper office of Charlie Hebdo; Christian churches attacked in multiple Nigerian cities on Christmas Day; Boston Marathon bombing; Peshawar, Pakistan school massacre; Boko Haram capture of 185 women after killing twenty-five men; multiple Jewish synagogue stabbings; multiple attacks by Abu Sayyaf in southern Philippines; nightclub massacre in Orlando, Florida; Bastille Day attack in Nice, France; cars driven into people on the Westminster Bridge and London Bridge; Palm Sunday church bombings in Alexandria, Egypt; Kizlyar Church shooting, Russia; Sri Lanka Easter church bombings, the most recent beheading of Samuel Paty, a middle school teacher in a Paris suburb. . . . And the blood continues to flow, from the violence of men!

Does this evident evil come from one source? Perhaps a country or religion comes to your mind? When we watch the footprint of terrorism, we begin to formulate an opinion about *who* is responsible for these attacks. There *are* certain regions and groups that perpetrate much of this destruction. *But the ultimate source of evil is not a human one.* In accordance with Scripture, in the same manner in which all good comes from the heart of God, all that is evil comes from the personification of evil—the fallen angel Lucifer, also called the Devil or Satan. *This is our real and eternal enemy.*

Many terrorists operate freely and out in the open. This is possible when the environment is lawless or lacks a stable civil government. Such was the case with Abu Bakr al-Baghdadi as he led his Islamic State jihadis attempting to set up a "caliphate" in portions of Syria. Terrorists operating in the open have been prevalent in other lawless regions including Somalia. At one critical time in the Horn of Africa, I was involved in coordinating significant medical services for people in desperate need.

In December 1992, with Somali clan-based warlords fighting, coupled with the worst drought in northeast Africa in a century, extreme famine conditions threatened one-fourth of Somalia's population. With no central government to speak of, security deteriorating throughout the country, and thousands of tons of international relief and food supplies stranded in warehouses in the port of Mogadishu, President George H. W. Bush ordered 28,000 US troops to join onsite UN troops in "Operation Restore Hope." He sent them to provide care and protection to the "innocents" and to participate in protecting the provision of famine relief. Bush initiated this in some coordination with Bill Clinton, who became president one month later in January 1993. It was into this milieu that I directed the charity I led to establish a major emergency relief campaign.

With both Dr. Jack Henderson, Dr. John Mulder, and other medical professionals on our team, as well as an ABC television crew and selected stakeholders, we first headed to Nairobi, Kenya. There were no commercial flights in or out of Somalia at that time, so we scheduled a private charter through the UN liaison office. Upon arrival in what is now called Aden Adde International Airport we taxied our two eight-passenger Cessna turboprops to the side of an open area. Three waiting vans received the significant cargo we off-loaded ourselves including personal gear, medical supplies, instruments, professional cameras, and sound equipment. With no formal entry procedure, we simply and swiftly exited through a gate on the east side of the airport and headed north on Jaziira Road toward central Mogadishu. Since there were no functioning hotels, at least safe ones, I had arranged for all of us to stay in a private rented compound with a dozen sparsely furnished rooms. There was a centralized latrine area and no operable kitchen, but we did have a makeshift eating area under an open-air canopy.

Surrounded by ten-foot high walls with barbed wire along the top, we could hear a range of disturbing sounds. The most regular and unnerving was gunfire, which could break out anytime in a twenty-four-hour period. The obsidian night sky punctuated with thousands of twinkling crystals reminded me that in spite of what we were in the middle of, God was in control.

Our first night's dinner and, in fact, our six remaining nights' dinners were the same. What they served was all that was readily available. From a huge metal pot, we scooped cooked white rice, taken from 50-kilogram sacks donated by international charities. This was complemented by abundant piles of cooked fresh lobster from the nearby Indian Ocean. And we washed it down with pitchers of sweet pineapple juice from trees growing outside of the destroyed central urban district. This surprise feast was brought in by armed "Technical"[2] every evening around 8:00 p.m. These vehicles became our primary mode of transportation for the week. Rented for $100 per day, they were driven by a daredevil-cowboy with an even crazier dude operating the large tripod machine gun mounted in the back. We fit into the sides as best we could. Consider that the streets and checkpoints were full of Humvees and armored military vehicles and you can appreciate the conditions we were in.

Each morning at 07:00 ("oh seven hundred") we would meet at the UNOSOM[3] headquarters. The gathering included ninety-plus humanitarian workers, medical personnel, and multinational military liaison personnel. The meeting was presided over by a US full-bird colonel who would update us on the current security situation, and ask each charity to identify what their mission was for the day and what locations they needed to travel to. His staff would mark the details on a whiteboard, including our all-important projected wrap-up time so they could track our safe return. Then his staff would assign military vehicles to accompany us.

Our mission was to conduct mobile medical clinics to wandering groups of displaced villagers in more remote locations as far south as Kismaayo, though we did conduct one clinic north in Wanlaweyn. The southern areas, furthest from the capital, were especially dicey so we were given both forward and rear protection vehicles with mounted M249 light machine guns. Our first day out, we had not driven two kilometers past the "Green Zone"[4] when a hail of cross fire with visible tracers careened in front of our caravan of six. The staff sergeant driving the lead vehicle braked for a moment, waiting for a "clearing," then accelerated, and we all followed at double time.

Each mobile clinic operation was an exhausting marathon of all-consuming focus, from the moment of our arrival to two hours before sundown. This allowed sufficient time to break down our operation and get back safely. We set up in preassigned locations, mostly abandoned shells of buildings with tarpaulins providing some relief from the blazing African sun. Lines of sick women and children had been waiting for hours before our arrival. Where were the men? As we disembarked and organized the health stations, young men came out of the scrub and started roughly pushing aside those in line to get in line themselves. It was difficult to contain our disgust. We dispatched one military escort with each medical staff and reestablished order.

Dr. Jack served as the enforcer, with an interpreter translating his words. "Hey, get your hands off her. . . . I said back off. . . . Is something wrong with you? . . . If *you* want us to help *you*, then stand in *that* line now and wait!" Dr. John was busy organizing the sequential health stations, each with a

US troops queueing patients

separate purpose, under the tarpaulin and getting the right medical supplies to their destination. "Put those medicines here, and ask our military escorts to place one guard here. . . . Medic, please assist me with getting their vitals when the patients start coming. . . . Bashir, are you translating for us? OK, then please be sure you *carefully* ask them what is wrong. . . . I may ask questions which will need to be translated. OK, let 'er rip, let's begin."

The triaged patients from Group 1, who had been baking in the hot sun, began to limp or shuffle in. Anemia, pneumonia, diarrhea, and measles were rampant. We learned the gut-wrenching news that one man had walked one hundred miles with his four children to get to this transitory health station—and that two of his children had died on the way. Everyone on the medical team gave every ounce of their energy and compassion, as well as *all* our pharmaceuticals and medical supplies, before we left drenched with sweat and tired to the bone.

Throughout the demanding hours of our medical clinic we also anticipated acute hunger. Other team members set up an adjacent feeding station under a tarpaulin. Children were first, the youngest receiving a high nutrition "wet" meal to allow ease of swallowing and to minimize agitation in their empty stomachs. Mothers and the elderly received the remainder of what food we had available.

Mom feeds her baby   *Boy enjoys some food*

This environment was one of the toughest I had encountered in decades of global humanitarian service. My journal summarized: *hot, dusty, dangerous, difficult, sobering, and sad . . . yet honorable, rewarding and most certainly memorable.* Americans will also remember the incident (and later movie) of "Black Hawk Down" when US public opinion turned against our continued efforts in Somalia. The evening news showed brazen Somalis dragging the bodies of eighteen dead US servicemen out of two downed Black Hawk helicopters. Armed rebel groups such as SSDF, SNM, SPM, and warlord generals like Mohamed Farrah Aidid and Ali Mahdi Muhammad, fighting the military junta of Siad Barre created instability that years later still exists in some form to this day. Al Shabaab is the latest iteration of terrorists making life miserable in Somalia and in that entire region of Africa.

It is hard to fully grasp that just across the southwestern border of Somalia is the democratic country of Kenya. Like every postcolonial African country, there have been power struggles and endemic inequities in the systems of government that are still being addressed. Yet for being next-door neighbors, these two countries seem to exist on separate planets. Located on the equator, Kenya is a land of enchantment with so much beauty and blessing. I have enjoyed many trips here, including a memorable mission trip and safari with my then-adolescent daughters, Chelsea and Misty.

Kenya boasts the vast awesomeness of the great Serengeti Plain and a large portion of the Rift Valley, filled with every form of wildlife— lions, leopards, cheetahs, elephants, rhinos, giraffes, zebra, wildebeest, ostriches, and a symphony of birds in every color. There is the majesty of snow-covered Mount Kilimanjaro, the strength and bright colors of the lowland Masai villages, and the breathtaking green of the Kikuyu Highlands. Take in Lake Nakuru teeming with thousands of pink flamingos, schedule time to view nature at safari parks like Amboseli National Park or Masai Mara National Reserve, grab a cool drink and a rest in the shade at Aberdare Country Club, or view the night grazing animals at The Ark Lodge. Or visit the family home of Karen Blixen— one of the pen names used by Danish Baroness Karen Christenze von Blixen-Finecke, author of *Out of Africa*. And nothing compares with the friendliness and hospitality of the Kenyan people. If you have the chance and have not been—come to Kenya!

Shifting gears, let me change just a few words from the first three sentences of this chapter: *The enemy* uses deception, intimidation, and violence in pursuit of a *spiritual* objective. The most effective *enemy* is a hidden one. He strikes at his victim's most vulnerable

Mount Kilimanjaro

point of access, while he is unaware and unguarded. "Are you aware of the spiritual battle being waged around you today? The truth is that although spiritual warfare is a major theme of the Bible, many of us gloss over it—or ignore it completely. But 80 percent of the synoptic gospels addresses the battle with evil spirits, and Jesus and his disciples set a clear example for believers. We cannot afford to practice a powerless Christianity in a fallen world."[5]

How does our enemy function? Scripture tells us directly who our mortal and eternal enemy is, and how to defeat him:

> *Put on the full armor of God, so that you can take your stand against the devil's schemes. For our struggle is not against flesh and blood, but against the rulers, the authorities, against the spiritual forces of evil in the heavenly realms.* (**Eph. 6:11–12**)

And no wonder, for Satan himself masquerades as an angel of light. It is not surprising, then, if his servants also masquerade as servants of righteousness. Their end will be what their actions deserve. **(2 Cor 11:14–15)**

You belong to your father, the devil, and you want to carry out your father's desires. He was a murderer from the beginning not holding to the truth, for there is no truth in him. When he lies, he speaks his native language, for he is a liar and the father of lies. **(John 8:44)**

Submit yourselves, then, to God. Resist the devil, and he will flee from you. **(Jas. 4:7)**

The first tactic in Satan's strategy of deception is to cause as much of humankind as possible to believe that he *does not exist.* Humanity sees and experiences evil everywhere. Yet, through lies and delusions, he convinces people not to recognize him as the source of evil, along with the dark angels from the spirit world which fell with him. Nonbelief is easily embraced by people in our postmodern, secular western societies who have removed or ignored any thought or concern for God. If any consideration at all is given to "the devil," they imagine him only as a mythical, comedic character with a red body and face and a goatee and tail, holding a pitchfork. Nonbelief is equally embraced by the majority of populations in communist and totalitarian countries that have been taught from birth, and therefore believe, that there is no God and certainly no devil. For the atheist, it is complete foolishness to entertain such a weak-minded position of superstition. There are billions of people in this category.

The second tactic in Satan's strategy of deception is directed toward those who *do* believe he exists. There are two broadly defined groups of people in this category. The first group comprises those who have yielded themselves to Satan's service and lordship. These human believers in Satan take on various roles of spiritual warfare against Christians and those who are still seeking to find God. They include witches and warlocks, spiritists and occultists, mediums and fortune-tellers, voodooists and Satan worshippers, to name some. The second group is large indeed—comprised of billions of people in every major world religion, including "nominal" individuals who attend Christian churches, as well as those with no specific religious affiliation. These persons believe in *a devil*, but have no knowledge of his purpose or how to deal with him. They go about life on a wing and a prayer, just hoping that nothing bad happens to them. They have no clue about the activities of this enemy or how Scripture describes him or his purpose.

Unfortunately, this category also includes a large swath of the Christian faith community. "Evangelical theologians, to the extent that they deal with the spirit world at all, tend to spend their time discussing whether or not demons exist today. Often, they follow liberal thinking by suggesting that what the New Testament portrayed as demons was merely pre-scientific understanding of what we know now were psychological problems. Many pastors join them, eliminating spiritual warfare from their agendas. In addition, evangelical scholars and pastors have bought into the secular assumption that emotional problems are all psychological not spiritual."[6]

Satan and his minions are liars and murders (John 8:44, 1 John 3:12); blind and bind the minds of unbelievers (2 Cor. 4:4); deceive like wolves in sheep's clothing (Matt. 7:15); falsely produce signs and wonders (2 Thess. 2:9); tempt people to sin (2 Cor. 11:3); choke faith and pluck God's word out of people's hearts (Rom. 10:17); cause some illnesses and disease (Acts 10:38); and accuse believers before God (Rev. 12:10).[7] "The enemy has no problem with those who believe in his existence, but do not practice against him. He has the most trouble with those who have correct assumptions and oppose him actively—those who believe he is alive and well and who practice setting people free from Satanic activity."[8]

The third tactic in Satan's strategy of deception is focused on believing Christians who have an understanding that he is the enemy *and* understand his purpose and devices. I put myself in this category, as perhaps you do. Nevertheless, this angel of darkness has the devious capacity to undermine our walk with God. So long as we follow the guidelines of Scripture—staying in close fellowship and communion with our Father, through His Son, empowered by the Holy Spirit, and exercising the authority given to us—we safely live under the covering of his wing. But Satan understands our proneness to wander. His three most effective areas of attack against believers are *fear, isolation,* and *doubt.* We must follow the exhortation, "Do not be anxious about anything, but in every situation by prayer and petition, with thanksgiving, present your requests to God. And the peace of God, which transcends all understanding, will guard your hearts and your minds in Christ Jesus" (Phil. 4:6–7).

When we wander, anxiety turns to *fear.* And fear is a sign that we are no longer living in faith, trusting completely in the sovereignty of God. *Isolation* is an especially effective tool to break us down. There are eighty-one separate Scripture verses where God assures us that he will always be with us! One of my favorites is: "Be strong and courageous. Do not be afraid or terrified because of them, for the LORD your God goes before you; he will never leave you nor forsake you" (Deut. 31:6). But if we take our eyes off of God's promises we feel alone and Satan then attacks our heart, mind, and will mercilessly. *Doubt* has been with us from the garden of Eden. We doubt because we believe the lie. "Did God *really* say, 'You must not eat from *any* tree in the garden?'" And then, "But did God say, 'You must not eat fruit from the tree that is in the *middle* of the garden, and you must not touch it, or you will die?'"

(Gen. 3:1, 3, emphases added). Today that might sound like, "Don't I deserve more than what I am getting now?" "Haven't I sacrificed enough and should be free to have a little fun?" or, "What will a little [fill in the blank] hurt me?" *This is what we understand to be spiritual warfare.*

> *The enemy will often use places of wounding as occasions to oppress us; the same holds true for brokenness. In fact, it is more common to find spiritual warfare in broken places because the chasm in the heart and soul provides a place for the enemy to do his work. He is a divider after all; his main work is to divide man from God, man from one another, and man from himself.*[9]

> *The enemy can find all our dark sides and make us bleed if we're not careful.*[10]

While there are many good books on this topic, I commend to you the reading of one in particular, written by my former professor, Charles H. Kraft, *The Evangelical's Guide to Spiritual Warfare: Scriptural Insights and Practical Instruction on Facing the Enemy.*

I end this chapter on Satan separating man from one another with a personal story. A number of my friends are named Paul. I have other international friends named Pablo, Paulo, and Pavel. Whether English, Spanish, Portuguese, or Russian, every one of them is a great guy. My dear friend Paul Thompson (from Carlsbad, California) and I have a relationship spanning more than forty years. Lord, are we that old! We met in our twenties as wet-behind-the-ears new employees of the same organization. Over time we've supported each other in that organization, were competitors in rival organizations, and for one stretch of years even jointly founded our own consulting company. Paul and I have socialized together in many contexts. On one occasion,

I still remember us singing old songs, a little too loudly, after a few too many margaritas. We have traveled in similar places, worked on grants and projects together and climbed our respective ladders of success.

For a couple of decades, we scheduled an annual retreat to share our life journey, made God-honoring plans and commitments, and prayed for each other. I recall one such time when we went to Mohonk Mountain House in New Paltz, New York, in the Hudson Valley. My journal confirmed: *We reviewed last year's goals to realize some had not been fulfilled, and some were too general.* As we shared and prayed throughout that weekend we established new commitments and a renewed dependency on God to achieve them. Having an accountability partner is so important.

We've also been through dark times and dark places with each other. A great honor yet deep sadness we share is having given the eulogy at each of our child's untimely death—Paul's son Blake at age twenty-six on June 28, and my daughter Bristol at age ten on July 25, twenty-one years apart. We both know that the five stages of grief don't just end in a linear progression at "acceptance," the fifth stage. In some capacity, we will grieve to our grave until we see our loved ones again. For one who does not know Christ, this statement is fantasy. For we who have encountered the living Christ, our pain and loss is a transitory condition!

Could a solid relationship like mine and Paul's ever be challenged? It has, and we were smart enough to recognize it. In truth, Paul and I are at completely opposite poles when it comes to politics. We generally avoid this divisive topic. But there have been occasions when each of us couldn't help ourselves. Like the time I sent him a goading text during a presidential election year saying our family's votes would cancel out his family's votes. Or the time he called while driving, after listening to a news item, and blurted out, "Ralph, you can't really tell me you are proud of this guy!"

This area of division is where Satan is particularly effective with believers. Each of us has closely held beliefs and an overall worldview that we are now comfortable with. Politics in the US has gone from divisive to hyper-crazy and vicious. Of course, there are many other issues that people differ on and disagree over. One insight from Scripture is particularly helpful.

"A person may think their own ways are right, but the LORD weighs the heart" (Prov. 21:2).

One thing I am certain of regarding our human condition: the systemic presence of sin, brokenness, and separation from God. It prevails in every living creature on earth—every race, every country, every generation. Humankind has been hating and killing each other since Cain and Abel—every "color" combination and every political rivalry possible, including *intra-race* conflicts (Hutu and Tutsi, Chinese and Japanese, Arapaho and Comanche); *intra-creed* conflicts (Shia and Sunni, Catholics and Protestants). There is an endless list of "inter" conflicts also: Hindu Tamils and Buddhist Sinhalese; Afghans and Soviets; Saudis and Yemenis; drug cartels and civilization; World War I and II; Korean War; Vietnam; Turks and Armenians; Slavs, Bosnians, and Croats; Palestinians and Jews; Iranians and Iraqis. This list could go on for pages. Do a web search on "war in . . ." then insert any region or time period. The results are mind-numbing!

Speakers must know their audience. Businesses must know their customers. Military strategists and Christian intercessors alike must know their enemy. We have already identified who our *real* enemy is. So how must this change our treatment of each other? We will always disagree on something—as individuals, with our spouses, amongst friends and coworkers, between nations. God alone brings true peace and justice. "The heart is deceitful above all things and beyond cure. Who can understand it?" (Jer. 17:9). "Turn from evil and do good; seek peace and pursue it" (Ps. 34:14). "Learn to do right; seek justice.

Defend the oppressed" (Isa. 1:17). Prayerful believers in Christ believe these truths of Scripture. But how do we effectuate them in a pluralistic and hostile society?

Any lasting solution to conflict or disagreement will not be a political one, but rather a spiritual one. Hatred, racism, murder, vandalism, destruction, drive-by looting . . . are all the work of Satan! A third of the angels of heaven fell with Lucifer when he was banished from God's presence. Satan and his demonic hosts are real, operating below the surface of people's everyday awareness, hiding in the shadows and operating in our confusion and fear. His work is to undermine everything God is doing in us and through us. "The weapons we fight with are not the weapons of the world. On the contrary, they have divine power to destroy strongholds" (2 Cor. 10:4). We begin by realizing our true enemy is the enemy. And then we trust in almighty God.

Call on me in the day of trouble; I will deliver you, and you will honor me. (**Ps. 50:15**)

Chapter 10
WANDERING

All that is gold does not glitter, not all those who
wander are lost; the old that is strong does not wither,
deep roots are not reached by the frost.
— *J. R. R. Tolkien*

There is a gloriously cool breeze whispering through the Jeffrey pines and red firs here in Mammoth Lakes, California on this August day where I chose to start writing this chapter. With it, the scented smell of the conifer forest. My friend Lorin Ganske invited me to join a group of guys from his church, all of us eager to get out of our COVID-19 sequestration that had dragged on far too long. We each made the six-hour journey up from Southern California, where we had been sweltering in over 100ºF temperatures for weeks. Everyone was out mountain biking, fishing, or hiking. I decided to use the quiet time to exercise my fingers on my mini Dell laptop.

The motivation to write this book was borne from profound thankfulness to God, for his provision and mercy, at every incredible stage of my life. I've shared a few of these stages already. This one is the hardest to capture. Literary parity would give voice to multiple perspectives that could be heard. Since that is not possible, you're stuck with *my* attempt to describe this period of wandering in a condensed but forthright manner. Throughout this time, I knew that I was God's son, still saved by grace. Yet, I became estranged . . . and lost, as a result of my own decisions. This season wedged open greater access to me by our devious enemy. God was always with me, but I did not always recognize his presence—lost in my own pain and internal issues.

It is my profound belief that many of you have or will find yourself in a spiritual wilderness *sometime*. My reason for believing this is based on Scripture. "I do not understand what I do. For what I want to do I do not do, but what I hate I do. . . . For I know that good itself does not dwell in me, that is, in my sinful nature. For I have the desire to do what is good, but I cannot carry it out. For I do not do the good I want to do, but the evil I do not want to do—this I keep on doing. . . What a wretched man I am! Who will rescue me from this body that is subject to death? Thanks be to God, who delivers me through Jesus Christ our Lord!" (Rom. 7:15, 18–19, 24–25).

My presumptive starting point was already described in the preface: *So, we're going along doing just fine, thank you. Then "it" happens. "It" is not the same for each of us. "It" may be betrayal, divorce, cancer, death of a loved one, financial ruin, or the feeling that we have lost our inner compass. But whatever "it" is will most certainly strike at your heart in a profound way. We become disoriented, find ourselves in a wilderness of self-doubt, on a darkened path, suddenly not sure if . . . if we're on the right path, if we should have taken the road less traveled. We wonder if God has abandoned us because we were stupid enough to get involved in or involved with [fill in the blank]. Each one sneaks up and bites us.* So, let me share a summary of my period of wandering.

I was working at home one afternoon when my wife took a phone call. From her furtive behavior walking to another room to speak, I knew something was wrong. When she returned, I asked, "Who was that on the phone?" She told me the name of a contractor who had finished his work in our backyard well over two months ago. Then I asked, "*Why* would he be calling, and w*hy* would he would be calling *you*?"

She hesitated, then after what seemed like an eternity, but likely was only five seconds, she let me know that she had been intimate with him. She began, "I haven't been happy in our relationship for some time." The path of our conversation brought me an increasing jolt of emotional pain with each passing sentence. I normally react to most things quickly, but I was stunned and said very little, at least very little that was coherent. "Please sit down," she continued. When she said this, I knew this conversation was going to get more complicated. Before *she* sat down, she grabbed a telephone book (which still existed in those days)! With great emotion in staccato bursts, she proceeded to explain that she had *also* been involved in a more serious relationship with the neighbor directly across the street . . . for about eighteen months. There was a period of silence as I let this all sink in. She started to speak again and her voice grew louder as she flipped haphazardly through the yellow pages, looking for the attorney section. She advised me, with some certainty, that she was not interested in counseling and wanted a divorce.

When confronted with irritating, unexpected, or frustrating things I can become fairly animated. For serious or life-threatening matters, I am strangely calm and, externally at least, in control. This certainly seemed to fall into the latter category. I told her, "I need some time to think and will be back." After quietly leaving the house, I drove to a park close to my home and was gone for about two hours. During this time, I thought, reasoned, and argued with myself. My mind lurched over the years of our marriage, replaying many scenarios. I prayed. The tears stung my eyes. The Psalms, again, became my familiar balm. When I returned, I had decided to go away for a while before making any drastic or lasting decisions. My time of reflection and seeking God turned out to be for two weeks. I rented a cabin in the mountains near Big Bear, packed my bags, and said a tearful goodbye to my three young daughters. I cannot recall the last thing I did or said to my wife.

By the time I came home, I had outlined a plan in my head, to the extent that it would work. I greeted my daughters with a big hug and kiss, then requested some privacy. "I need to talk with mom."

"OK Daddy, can we play when you are finished?" they sweetly asked, assuming everything was back to normal.

"Sure, my angels," I smiled. I had no idea how I would pull off this feat of determination.

It took some doing, but I convinced my wife that we *needed* to go to counseling even if we didn't stay together. In a reasonable amount of days, we selected someone we both felt comfortable with. My overarching thought was that I loved my daughters with all my heart and did not want another man to raise them. I wanted to be the influence in their lives, and guide them to adulthood. Divorce situations with young children nearly always end in complex blended families, heartbreak, and the infliction of deep, lifelong wounds.

At this juncture, we were also on year nine and six months of my oldest daughter Bristol's degenerative neurological disease. She died at ten years and three months. The onerous burden of a decade of doctor visits, surgeries, therapy and more therapy, fights with insurance companies, the unfair imbalance of time and attention paid to the ill one at the expense of the healthy ones, *all* took their toll on each of us. Then add to this, well-meaning friends who, presuming by now that Bristol was going to die, would ask questions like, "Have you considered donating her vital organs to a donor bank?" Or, "Why don't you have enough faith for her to be healed?" My response to this entire pile of crap was to suck it up and try harder . . . through counseling, at work, and with the family. My lifelong mantra is, "I *never* give up!"

One supreme irony of this situation hit me right between the eyes. With thanks to God, I had made it into my late forties, having traveled the world without succumbing to *the* most prevalent temptation faced by traveling men. *Not even once.* I'm sure there are temptations for traveling women, but I can't speak to this. In my experience, I had been propositioned or otherwise had access to commercial sex opportunities pushing 40 to 50 percent of the time. I'd sat at an empty table on the patio of the Serena Hotel in Nairobi when a woman silently slipped into the chair next to me and described how to pay the floor monitor for her to get up to my room. Having checked into the massive Rossiya Hotel off Moscow's Red Square, I had just put my key in the door of my room when the phone rang. When I answered, the female voice said, "Do you want good sex? Tell me and I will deliver her to your room. You want blonde? Da?" And after many years of service in central Vietnam, the provincial governor himself told me to select from one of the six to eight young women who served our meals and said he would send her to my room that evening.

To these opportunities and many more, I had said *no thank you* and avoided this area of sin. It was a gut punch to be staring infidelity in the face—after all I had avoided, by God's grace, for so many years.

Allow me now in a few paragraphs to compress multiple years of time, not in precise chronology, to describe many life dynamics which took place next. My daily existence meandered on, like walking in the grainy haze of a sandstorm. A series of transitions and crucible events made up the mosh pit of my life during this period. Just a few months into our marriage counseling, which of course also involved dealing with childhood and family-of-origin issues, our daughter Bristol died. We hadn't even scratched the surface of one issue. Now we were dragged into another black hole of complexity. Grief, sadness, pressure, regret, despair, anger, faith teetering like a tower in a hurricane, feeling sorry for myself . . . each played their part in this macabre symphony. Just two months later, an executive recruiter offered me a CEO position in Michigan. Having resigned my job to focus on my hemorrhaging family, coupled with the shame and awkwardness of living in eyesight of the perpetrator across the street, after a thorough interview process, I accepted the offer.

Grand Haven, Michigan is a quaint and pleasant community with a population just over 10,000. It was 2,136 miles from our home in greater Los Angeles *and* light years of difference in terms of culture and expectations. My intention was to continue counseling to pursue our most definite need for healing. But this small town was a fishbowl where everyone seemed to know everyone's business. *And* two of the primary counselors went to our church. *And* their office was on the church property! I was now a more visible Christian leader, so I did what I am good at: I stuffed it, sucked it up, and buried myself in my work.

This new global opportunity fed the passion and purpose I had been given by God, confirmed many times since accepting Christ as my savior. A fulfilling decade passed. I loved my work. It was also a great place for my daughters to grow up. My resume went from silver to platinum. Our marriage would never recover, though ironically everyone in that time and context thought we were a happy couple and an ideal family.

My daughters both completed high school, and each preferred to attend college in California. I began to plan for a transition after the rewarding and successful decade as CEO of this Michigan charity. I offered the board a two-year transition plan with three major initiatives to complete. This would have allowed me time to properly transfer my personal affairs smoothly. The board, dominated at this point by business men and women, opted for a generous two-year severance package and a quick transition of leadership. In retrospect, this was not a good decision, and was detrimental *both* to the organization *and* to our family's sense of equilibrium. But I landed on my feet. Again, I was contacted by an executive recruiter and offered a CEO position in L.A. We all decided to go back to the sunshine. But with it came the crushing traffic and the loss of community we greatly valued in West Michigan. No one anticipated the unexpected changes that lay ahead.

Starting a new job, in and of itself, is a challenge. Becoming the CEO of a historic rescue mission in the heart of skid row was especially difficult. The homeless population had swelled in Los Angeles, with nearly as many women and children as men. In doing an internet search we discovered seventy registered sex offenders within a few square blocks of our facility. Drug deals occurred regularly throughout the 'hood. Needles, stabbings, violence, rape—it was a dark place. No one was safe. On the home front I was still trying, and had initiated counseling for us, *yet again*. Despite years of effort the ultimate goal was slipping away.

During this period of time, as if things couldn't get any more complicated, I needed to move my ailing dad and increasingly *weird* mother across country to live closer to us in California. I didn't realize at first that "weird" included Alzheimer's. The process started with cleaning out decades of their accumulated junk. I listed and sold their house and car and got them relocated. After flying them from Hartford, Connecticut to Ontario, California, via Chicago O'Hare, I started another blizzard of responsibilities. They had to learn all the buttons and switches in their new house and car. I had to repetitively pattern their understanding of how to get them from point A to B. I reestablished all of their services and doctors and got them acclimated to their new life. Dad died six months later. This left me with a strangely non-grieving mother and a new monster creeping into her life—and therefore, mine. Early signs of dementia blossomed into a full-blown mess. It eventually became unbearable. I put her in a care facility. She died soon thereafter, a withered shell with a confused brain. I arrived at her death bed fifteen minutes too late. My head was pounding. I commend to you my previous (coauthored) book, *My Mother, Your Mama: Stories of Caring for an Aging Parent,*[1] for a more complete picture of my situation *and* the challenges so many of us experience in caring for an aging parent.

After four-and-a-half years I resigned my position, with mutual understanding and agreement. I pivoted quickly, *again*, and started my own company and leased an executive suite in Newport Beach, close to the John Wayne / Orange County Airport. Without missing a beat, Satan was whispering in my subconscious. "Didn't you make a commitment to raise your daughters?" *Why yes . . . I did.* "And you successfully completed this commitment?" *Well, college really is the beginning of adulthood.* "Didn't the intimacy in your marriage end years ago?" *Yes, it did.* "Don't you deserve better?" *Oh . . . uh, yeah . . . I guess so.* "What do you want to do with the rest of your life, Ralph?" *Just get away and try something new.* After more counseling and moving out, then back, and out again, over a period of additional months I finally, and with consternation, decided to make a permanent change. I moved to our condo in Palm Desert "to start over." So much for the tough guy who never gives up. I filed for divorce. Alone is a vulnerable place to be.

For the next five years I pretty much did what I felt like doing. Always the entrepreneur, I created a number of commercial opportunities. I stayed busy, but I was not centered in God's will. Predictably, most of my efforts were not that successful. I vividly recall feeling deep sadness during a cool, rainy night in my hotel room in Mexico City, having spent too much time and money on an initiative which had just been turned down. I urgently sought God, but there was silence. Then I plunged into a variety of consulting gigs, and was able to throw enough on the wall for some of it to stick. With a tendency toward multitasking I was able to juggle many spinning plates on multiple spindles. I engaged in a series of relationships, none of which lasted—and more importantly, did not honor God. So, still running from myself and my pain, I decided to travel—for interest, not obligation. I went many places and did many things.

"The penalty for trifling with the Holy Spirit is breach of fellowship. For a while, the friends of the offender may not notice that he no longer walks with God. For a while, the offender himself may be unaware of his breach of fellowship with God. The eyes are accustomed themselves to walking in the twilight of the sun that has set. But when judgment comes, the only one who has trifled with God begins to realize that it is chilly after the sun has set, that he walks alone, and that he is stumbling in murky darkness."[2] As the Son began to shine again, God used two places in particular to break through the spiritual and emotional barriers I had erected.

I always loved the Cotswolds and have traveled there a number of times. This beautiful and quintessentially English region covers more than eight hundred square miles encompassing portions of five counties—Gloucestershire, Oxfordshsire, Warwickshire, Wiltshire, and Worcestershire. Nowhere else does the rolling landscape and the limestone manors and estates blend so magnificently. Little villages like Chipping, Campden, Bourton-on-the-Water, Stow-on-the Wold, and Bibury for me were places of respite and wonder. I gravitated toward the Oxford region and often stayed at a bed and breakfast just off the River Thames. Often, I would walk to Christ Church, at St. Aldate's on the Oxford University campus. Founded in 1546, this historic 175 acres in the central city is a haven of rest and academic excellence. Often, I would pray sitting on the grass under a tree in their expansive, well-groomed acreage. I encourage anyone who has not visited the beautiful Cotswolds region to do so.

I wasn't just a tourist, though. Thankfully, I started journaling again, thinking and praying more intently. There *were* flickers of moments when my prayers pierced the darkness. For a while longer, I kept my metaphorical head down and continued wandering. All the while God never left my side.

Paris is also a place I love to visit. I didn't cut corners this time, and used my "genius" status on Booking.com to reserve a room at the Marriott on the Champs-Élysées, just a stone's throw from the Arc de Triomphe. Having been here before, I focused on what I preferred rather than following the tourist map. I always enjoy the Louvre on Rue de Rivoli. The art is truly inspiring. I'd also stop midway over the Ponte des Arts pedestrian bridge spanning the River Seine to think and reflect, watching the peaceful water pass under my feet. Here too, I reached out to my Lord. At my lowest point, all I could pray was, "Father, please don't let me go."

Something stirred, and it prompted me to walk to the Ile de la Cité, where this island of fifty-six acres is graced with the renown La Cathédrale Notre-Dame de Paris, Our Lady of Paris. The magnificent bells were chiming as I arrived. My visit, of course, was before the tragic fire of April 15, 2019 which destroyed the vaulted ceiling, the vulnerable timber spirelet, wooden roof, and some of the invaluable historical icons and art. On this occasion, I arrived in time for the 11:30 a.m. international mass, giving me opportunity to draw on my three years of French in high school. *C'est bon.*

I felt compelled, then, to visit the Sacré-Coeur Basilica (the sacred heart—of Jesus) in the Montmartre district. In both places of worship, I asked God to show me the way home. He did! My mind drifted to my mother's abject rejection of the Catholic church. I thought too of some of my Protestant colleagues who held prideful and condescending positions on Catholicism. Did God somehow skip over his redemptive work on earth until 1517, the occasion of Martin Luther's 95 Theses at Wittenberg? In my experience, he certainly had not.

Almost as if wanting to get as high up toward the heavens as possible, I took the two elevators needed to reach the 108th story to the observation deck of the Eiffel Tower. It was about 11:00 p.m. I walked slowly, repeatedly, around the entire 360-degree panorama, watching the twinkling lights of Paris. I wrestled with my sense of disorientation, thinking about the years the locusts had eaten . . . and realizing God promised that He would restore them (Joel 2:25). I thought about many things and asked for forgiveness. I stayed until the last run of the down elevators at 12:45 a.m. It was time to get home . . . and get right with God.

Many of my friends and associates hit the wall somewhere, unexpectedly. For some it was in response to their *own* unexpected and debilitating illnesses. For some the death of a family member was just *too much*. Crisis with a wayward child had derailed some. Many experienced a devastating loss of income, their financial security out the window—or down the toilet, as the case may be. Others were just sick to death of being on the hamster wheel. Others came to the sobering realization that their spouse was no longer the same person they first married. For just about all of us . . . looking into the mirror at the wrinkled face of our mortality sucks!

What about you? What event or circumstance in your life has put you in a position of vulnerability, discouragement, or shame? I know from experience that our enemy is cunningly able to reach us at our greatest point of vulnerability. He uses the same lies and trickery that successfully tripped up our ancestors Adam and Eve. A foolish couple? We would have done the same! Satan today asks us questions that cause us to doubt ourself and to question God. Subtly he suggests a divergent path that leads away from God, from his grace and provision. If that is you right now, fight it with all your might. Return to God's Word. Read it often and trust in his promises! (I would value hearing from you via the contact information provided at the end of the book, if you'd care to do so, on this topic or any in this book.)

I admire and respect those people of faith who trust in God for their *entire* lives and are faithful throughout their journey. They never experience the perplexing path of the prodigal. Let's face it, some people are saints. Many of us are not! My message for those in this latter category is that God loves you. And he will most assuredly welcome you back if you want to be back. Few books explain this truth more profoundly that Henri Nouwen's *The Return of the Prodigal Son: A Story of Homecoming*: "Here the mystery of my life is unveiled. I am loved so much that I am left free to leave home. The blessing is there from the beginning. I have left it and keep on leaving it. But the Father is always looking for me with outstretched arms to receive me back and whisper in my ear, 'You are Beloved, on you my favor rests.'"[3]

Chapter 11
HIDDEN OR TRANSPARENT

Truth at last cannot be hidden. . . . Nothing is hidden under the sun. — ***Leonardo da Vinci***

"*Every saint has a past, and every sinner has a future.*" It's a good opening line for a presentation to a men's conference or even a motivational sermon in church. The theme would eventually touch on the bones in our closet; the inevitable failings that we all try to hide. And for the believer in Christ whose sin has been confessed and nailed to the cross, it is a reminder that we are saved by grace through faith (Eph. 2:8). This line, written by nineteenth-century Irish playwright and poet Oscar Fingal O'Flahertie Wills Wilde, is only the second half of the sentence. His complete thought is, "The *only difference* between the saint and the sinner *is that* every saint has a past, and every sinner has a future." That changes the meaning altogether!

Whether we are considered by our contemporaries to be a either sinner or a saint is irrelevant. God sees and knows our hearts. So much of what is external does not reflect what truly *is*. When compared to our heavenly Father, we all have sinned and fall short of his glory. Therefore, we cannot exhibit the holiness God requires to live eternally in his presence. Innately and inherently we each know and feel a sense of being incomplete and disconnected from something greater than ourselves. Which is why the sacrificial death and resurrection of

Jesus, paying the price for our sin, is such an amazing and precious gift.

Since the garden of Eden, humankind has been trying to hide from God. It's such a silly and pointless thing to attempt when we fully understand who God truly is. "'Who can hide in secret places so that I cannot see them?' declares the LORD. 'Do I not fill heaven and earth?'" (Jer. 23:24). Psalm 139 explains that my Creator has searched me and knows me, knows my thoughts, and knows even when I sit or get up. He knows what I am going to say even before it is spoken. He saw my unformed body and knew how my days would unfold before one of them came to be. "Nothing in all creation is hidden from God's sight. Everything is uncovered and laid bare before the eyes of him to whom we must give account" (Heb. 4:13). Proverbs 28 also tells us that when we try to hide our sin we will not prosper, but when we renounce our sin, we will find mercy. And this unequivocal truth, "The LORD searches every heart and understands every desire and every thought" (1 Chr. 28:9b). So why do we do it? Why do we try to hide?

> *The Genesis story attributes the fall of man to the lying and deceit of the Serpent, and the Revelation predicts that all liars shall have their lot in the lake of fire, the second death. The Ten Commandments condemn false witness, and the Lord told Moses and the children of Israel directly, "neither lie to one another" (Lev. 19:2). The Apostle Paul echoes the same word: "Do not lie one to another" (Col. 3:9); and "Therefore, putting away falsehood, let everyone speak the truth with his neighbor" (Eph. 4:25). The Psalms condemn lying, and so do the Proverbs. The Prophets warn against it, and so do the Apostles. The references to lying in the Bible are too numerous for comment.*[1]

We lie to gain something that we know is illegitimate—contravening God's law or men's laws. Then we hide and obfuscate.

Our world, from the fall in Eden until the day when the names written in the book of life are revealed, is under the control of the *father of lies*. Therefore, hiding is endemic and universal. This is easier to comprehend when considering the unregenerate world at-large. Yet even the discerning believer in Christ struggles with this. We understand that the guideposts of Scripture speak plainly. But our inborn tendency is to avert our spiritual eyes from God and pretend, or at least not think about, this truth. We know in our inner self when we are doing something wrong. Human knowledge calls this our *conscience*. Spiritual wisdom attributes this to the conviction of the Holy Spirit.

We have briefly considered a life that avoids transparency and tries to hide, on an individual level. Now let's look at this from a transnational perspective, and then finally, interpersonally. If the entire world and its inhabitants—our human race—is infected with this sickness, then we should be able to make an important deduction when considering the actions of the nations and their leaders.

There exists, without doubt, corruption, lies, and purposely hidden events and decisions in every political system, spanning every period of human history. People in power, above all else, do everything they can to retain their power. And the predictable result for the subjects or citizens of those political systems is that they most often come out on the short end of the stick. What we have then, in this fallen world, are degrees of broken systems with various gradations of transparency or secrecy. In my global travels, I have had the unique privilege of being allowed access to some of the most repressive regimes on the planet, where hiding the truth and hiding *from* truth prevails.

On two occasions I have traveled to the Democratic People's Republic of Korea (DPRK), aka North Korea. Additionally, I have worked for years in and through Christian ministries and humanitarian organizations who served the suffering people inside this hermit kingdom. Trust me when I tell you, there is nothing *democratic* about this place, and it sure as hell (exists) is not run by *the people*.

One project I coordinated during a time of significant hunger and famine in North Korea was the purchase of a ten-boxcar trainload of bulk wheat. This complex initiative, funded by donations from South Korean churches, involved in-person purchase through an intermediary Beijing bank, and logistics coordination managed out of Dandong, Liaoning Province, China. The Yalu River (also called the Amrok River) provides the heavily guarded border between China and North Korea. Four hours from Dandong to the north by car is a particular crossing site where many brave North Koreans have risked their lives attempting a dangerous flight to freedom. Some made it; many others were caught and returned to severe punishment or death.

Do I imagine that *all* of the wheat got to the neediest people? Undoubtedly not, but some did. We presume much went to the military and ruling class. But we had confirmation, from some who successfully defected, that our efforts were a beacon of hope to those still suffering. The intricacies of God's ways are above our understanding. And important for us, this project created a bridge for future access. The invitation came through the DPRK Mission in New York, which required the approval of Pyongyang. I invited two businessmen and my global companion Dr. Jack. Our week-long trip to North Korea would focus on medical assistance.

November is not the best time of year to visit this climate and region. We actually had to get through our own delay with an ice storm at Chicago O'Hare. Dr. Jack and I met our two businessmen traveling companions—Bud Hoffman, who was with me in South Africa, and Jerry Horne—at Narita International in Japan arriving in the evening. Since our flight to Beijing wasn't until 10 a.m. the next morning I had booked rooms at the Radisson Narita. At dinner we reviewed what best we could ascertain was our schedule. This was not transparently communicated to us. For sure we were going to see what they wanted us to see. "Listen guys, one likely factor which will affect our visit is we're arriving during the anniversary of the death of Kim Il-Sung, first head of the DPRK. He died of a sudden heart attack in 1994."

Jerry inquired, "When did this guy first become President, if that's what they call him?"

Since I reviewed the history before this trip I expounded, "He is now called 'Our Great Leader,' and officially took over in 1948. With the end of Japanese rule in 1945 there was a period of great suffering and chaos. This is usually the time when communist or socialist movements have the greatest opportunity."

Bud added, "From my reading, Kim's held a bunch of titles over the years: Premier, President, Leader of the Workers Party, General Secretary and Chairman."

"Wow," Jerry quipped, "He must have printed a lot of business cards."

Our four-hour flight to Beijing was uneventful. One of Jerry's China-based employees picked us up in their van and drove us directly to the DPRK Embassy in time to process our visa. We were warned it could take hours, but for some reason our delegation was expected and preapproved. My journal recorded: *We were in and out of there in TEN minutes!*

Next stop, the Air Koryo office to purchase round trip tickets. We headed for the airport and boarded the Russian Tupolev Tu-204-100B with a capacity for 222 passengers; the plane was full. The colors of green (military), black (business), and grey (mid-level officials) dominated the seating. I wrote in my journal: *Lord, go before us in a special way for these days ahead.* We were met by Mr. Jon and Mr. Pak (I will not give their full names) from the Ministry of Foreign Affairs who were our guides and *minders* for the duration. Before leaving the airport, security required us to leave our cell phones in their "care," to be picked up again on our departure. Jerry, especially, was not pleased with this demand.

Outside we were blasted with cold air, barren terrain, and muddy evidence of receding flooding. The ride to central Pyongyang took twenty minutes and we were surprised to discover upon arrival at the Taedonggang Hotel that our rooms and food would be fully covered by the "state." Despite the fact that I worked for a charity, with two important businessmen-donors in tow, I was considered "The Honored Chairman" and given Suite #203, a four-room monstrosity with a bedroom, sitting room, office, bathroom, *and* a foyer/hall way that could have accommodated a women's field hockey match. It was, *of course*, bugged for both sound and video.

No matter what time zone I am in, my body clock predictably wakes me in about five hours. As a result, I was showered, dressed, and out for an early morning walk, in the cold gray of Pyongyang. I have done this in every place on the planet. With no idea where I am going—I just figure it out. On this particular morning I walked past imposing buildings, built in Soviet-style dullness. Huge statues of important people to the regime watched us in silent menace. Turning toward the Taedong River I spent some time slowly walking out of the commercial district and toward a cluster of high-rise residences. Each unit had a small back porch piled high with cabbage. For sure, this represented enough future kimchi to feed an army.

Many residents of this elite, by-invitation-only capital city were on their way to work. Even though I was bundled up with a long wool coat, earmuffs, scarf, and gloves I was clearly recognized as a *foreigner*. And without question, I was being followed. My journal recorded my impression (and lucky for me, my journal remained in my possession!): *Bone chilling cold. Some street cars and buses. No personal autos. People waiting in lines with frosty breath. Everyone is walking silently with their eyes averted. Screaming silence.*

I will intentionally condense commentary on the remainder of this bizarre and unique trip. Much had hidden intent. On the political side of the visit, we were first brought to Mangyongdae Native House, birthplace of the Great Leader. It was well kept, with piped-in music and every bush in place amongst the manicured landscape.

This didn't hold a candle to our visit to what is now called Kumusan Palace of the Sun, where Kim Il-Sung is entombed in a glass mausoleum. Lines of weeping and wailing Korean women dressed in black, four and five abreast, stretched for what seemed like miles, anticipating

Kim Il-Sung, Pyongyang

their once-in-a-lifetime opportunity to view the Great Leader in repose. We were dropped off directly at the entrance stairs and ushered into the line of expressionless visitors. We passed crisply uniformed military at every turn, with somber music playing.

When we arrived in the "holy of holies," Kim lay in perpetual state, with dim red lighting and a hallowed hush in the high-ceilinged all-marble room. This commemorative event was videoed and we discovered ourselves on the morning news. We were later dropped off at Revolutionary Square with huge statues of Marx, Lenin, and the Great Leader, which towered over silent lines of workers waiting for their early evening bus home to their state-owned apartments.

Following this impressionable experience, we were escorted to the Three Revolution Exhibition—a large Smithsonian-like complex. This large facility showcased the three-revolutions of the Great Leader—ideological, technical, and cultural. To emphasize the first revolution, we were "allowed" to visit the 152-foot statue of Kim Il-Sung as well as the 170-meter Juche Tower built with 75,000 tons of granite. This massive edifice glorifies the official ideology of North Korea,"self reliance" or juche in Korean. The sign at the entrance read, "Man is the master of everything."

We were asked to sign one of the fancy guestbooks. I wrote, "May God bless Korea and reunite its people." This was translated on the spot by an observer and brought a smile to our guides. It was written with intentional neutrality. If only years later, visiting American and University of Virginia student Otto Warmbier could have exercised a bit of caution, he would *not* have been sent back home in a vegetative state. Later, upon examination it was confirmed that the torture inflicted on him included his bottom teeth being rearranged by a pair of pliers, then pushed back into his jaw haphazardly.

I haven't yet mentioned that throughout these site visits our *minders* were effusively, perpetually commenting on "the Great Leader this" and "the Great Leader that." This statue was the tallest in the world; this building was the best in the world; this monument was the biggest in the world. Somewhere during our tours, I heard one of my traveling colleagues mutter under his breath the *more earthy* version of, "This is bovine feces." At one point, after listening to so much about how the DPRK hates America, Dr. Jack burst out in uncharacteristic frustration, "Then why did you invite us here?" My journal recalls, *You Lord,* are *the only true Great Leader, the almighty God, King of Kings—may your kingdom be established forever and your light shine here in this place. This god-man worshipping place is one of the most unreal experiences I've ever had! Thank you for this opportunity, because I have a better understanding of how to pray.*

On the cultural side, we were brought to Cheang Gwang Kindergarten. The young kids were so cute, but their programmed musical production and dance routine were painful to watch. Standing rigidly, some belted out patriotic choruses, while others did acrobatics with military precision; then they all sat down in unison.

One day as we were walking in the city, an orderly group of young children, with teachers guiding, stopped in front of us and belted out a song in unison. We presumed this was more instilled patriotism.

Kindergarten kids performing

We visited the Mansudae Arts Studio in the Pyeongcheon District to validate their claims to artistic expression. We were allowed to experience the religious "freedom" of this land with a visit to the Bongsu Church. We were greeted by the pastor. He shared, "This church was built in 1988, and is one of two 'Protestant' churches in Pyongyang. We have 322 *believers* (that was the intentional word used). And in the whole of the Democratic People's Republic of Korea there are ten thousand who believe in God." Something was distinctly *hidden* in this presentation.

Evening entertainment included a circus, in a theatre in the round, attended by mostly uniformed military. We also ate at the revolving restaurant on the forty-seventh floor of the Yanggako International Hotel. We were handed elaborate, multipage menus. Each in our group was given time to make a selection. Our choices ranged from fish to beef to traditional Korean. The process which followed made a statement. One by one we made our selections, but the response from the server was the same, "I'm sorry, we don't have that tonight." Finally, I said, "Well what *do* you have tonight?" In the end, all they had available was chicken. That is what all four Americans and our hosts had, no questions asked, no further comments made. Two of my colleagues just rolled their eyes at me silently.

Ryugyong Hotel, Pyongyang

We, of course, completed our humanitarian purposes. Meetings with the UNDP,[2] Public Health Ministry, Médecins Sans Frontières (Doctors without Borders), Taedonggang District Hospital, the Ansan Clinic, Hak San Cooperative Farm, and Port of Nampo where our containers of aid would be disembarked. Thinking that we could conduct any *transparent* humanitarian effort with full accountability was a pipe dream. But I had enough global experience to know that God opens and closes doors, gives favor, and even sometimes blinds the eyes of the oppressor so that his kingdom purposes are hidden from those who would block them. We had some minor "issues" getting out of the country, but we got out. I gave thanks to the Lord for his mercy and protection, with a now poignant understanding of how to pray more specifically for the people trapped within this hidden kingdom.

So much of the world's totalitarian regimes came out of the jumbled, satanically inspired brain of Karl Heinrich Marx. This 5' 9" ball of frazzled hair and beard was credited by some with being a philosopher, economist, historian, sociologist, political theorist, journalist, and socialist revolutionary. I consider this last moniker the correct one. His magnum opus, *Das Kapital*, was the flammable critique of capitalism which sent the world into a violent search for alleged social and economic justice where everyone is equal. "Imagine there's no heaven, it's easy if you try . . . imagine there's no countries, it isn't hard to do . . . nothing to kill or die for, and no religion too . . . imagine no possessions, I wonder if you can."[3] It all sounds like utopia, doesn't it? The center of this Marxist universe, until the rise of Maoist China, was the former Soviet Union, now Russia with a few other unofficial satellites. Today they are controlled by Vladimir Putin, buttressed with an occasional poisoning of his democratic opponents, just to keep a lid on things. I have traveled to Russia numerous times, as well as other former Soviet states. I'd like to tell you why.

The CoMission was a unique gospel movement inspired by the Holy Spirit at a divinely appointed time. The subtitle of the book about this movement states its purpose best: "The amazing story of eighty ministry groups working together to take the message of Christ's love to the Russian people."[4] After the disintegration of the Soviet Union there was a deep void of hope and meaning among the people, a hunger for what their souls lacked. God provided an opening for the Jesus Film Project to have a four-day audience in a convocation of public-school teachers held at the Pushkin Pioneer Palace. This event was a welcomed light shining in the darkness.

The result was an invitation by Alexi Brudnov, director of alternative education for the Ministry of Education in the former Soviet Union, to "an American team" that could "teach them about the Bible and a new course on Christian ethics and morals." Over a five-year period, this amazing invitation reached 42,000 teachers in 142 cities of the former USSR. I was the twelfth and final person invited to the executive committee.

My purpose was to coordinate "The Ministry of Compassion." As the CoMission penetrated the cities and towns across Russia, we found many people in need. My role included establishing a committee to respond to this need and to secure the tangible goods that would be shipped. By the culmination of this five-year long *kairos* opportunity, we were able to distribute about $18 million in material assistance to grateful recipients.

Our efforts for the people of this massive land, spanning ten time zones, continued for many years. Today under Putin, Russia has reemerged as a nation with a hidden, nefarious agenda. But in the decade of the 1990s and early 2000s God had opened a door. Subsequently, I hosted many trips with donors and Christian partners to bring hope and tangible aid to churches, hospitals, and a variety of missionary movements involved in evangelism and discipleship. Ukraine; Belarus; the Baltic states of Estonia, Latvia, and Lithuania; as well as the far eastern reaches of the Russian empire were blessed.

I vividly recall our visit to the village of Druzniya, in relative proximity to the Chernobyl nuclear disaster. As we talked to a group of women packed into a small gathering place. I asked, "What do you need most?" In Russian, with a translator, one woman then another said nearly the same thing. "My son (daughter) has cancer and we have no medicine. We need medicine for our children." A few pulled-out wrinkled pieces of paper, with tears in their eyes, told us that they had been given prescriptions for various medicines but there was nowhere to get them. In Vladimir we visited a shelter, called "a halfway house" for thirty abused and abandoned kids. They were given basic care and a roof over their heads. But at age eighteen, when they were "emancipated," they had nowhere to go and few skills that would give them a sustainable hope for the future.

As always, we visited some truly historic and lovely places. My favorite was Suzdal, part of the Golden Ring of ancient towns and the former "Holy See" of the Russian Orthodox church. At its center is the gold domed Cathedral of the Nativity, a stunning piece of architecture with its thirteenth-century frescos. Some fifty gorgeous churches and cathedrals exist in this small but historic city. It is a must-see for those traveling to Russia.

Of course, we spent time in the paradox called Moscow, the capital. On the one hand the city was filled with the grey, monolithic structures of Soviet bureaucracy. But the Kremlin, St. Basil's Cathedral, the Armory, Red Square, and even the GUM (shopping area) added color and a glimpse under the surface into the life and vibrancy of the Russian people.

There is *so much more* to see in this land of contrasts—the history and majesty of St. Petersburg and so many other places. My journal summarized the range of experiences: *Reflecting on our visits: resignation, cold and snowy, soviet communist insanity, no choices or options. Gilded history, but jaded present, listening to "How Great Thou Art" in Russian and English, bribes and corruption, a young, growing evangelical church, alcoholism and despair. But today as we depart, the sun is glistening off the gold towers of St. Basil's, just outside my*

St. Basil's Cathedral, Moscow

window. It's really breathtaking. Lord, thank you for giving me so many enriching experiences and opportunities to serve your people.

If we accept that hiding exists in every individual, then it is universal in every nation. And if we recognize that countries with leaders who have no allegiance to the redemptive presence of God in their laws and governance have citizenry who function in the same manner, then we should understand how this exacerbates the inevitability that these people groups will predominantly hide and lie. Logic would suggest our relations with such countries should be guarded. Trust but verify? In today's world, with Satan's time of temporary control growing ever shorter, I would say our relations with such countries like China and Russia should actually be distrust, verify, and still stay vigilant *at all times.*

Now let's cross the final bridge of understanding and address hiding at the interpersonal level. Consider a family unit. You likely can humorously recall when one of your young children tried to "sneak" something which you easily saw them do. The classic line is taking a cookie out of the cookie jar, that mom told them not to. Do cookie *jars* exist anymore? I was a lover of reading. When I was an adolescent, despite being told to be asleep by a certain time, I brought a flashlight to bed and read under the covers for hours.

Today, what battles do you wage with *your* kids or grandkids? The internet and smart phones add new complexities. More importantly, what battles are raging for *you* that you hide—too much time gaming or surfing the net, an illicit online relationship, pornography, gambling? Or perhaps a myriad of other things that are not connected to the internet? Think more about your immediate family, your extended family, your neighbors, your friends at church. What are you hiding from them? And what of your relationship to God? What actions have you "averted your eyes" from or tried not to think about, that you know *full well* God is aware of? This is an important reality I had to grapple with as God brought me back from my period of wandering. You can do the same!

A topic that is much too important to ignore, but much too complex to properly address here, is the connectivity between hiding and *shame*:

> *Shame is debilitating. It ruins relationships, thwarts growth, and destroys hope. It can masquerade as various problems—guilt, envy, pride, resentment—but until you heal the core issue, freedom will remain out of reach . . . Both guilt and shame are strong emotions that you must acknowledge and deal with for your relationships to go well. To manage your guilt, you must do things differently. Being honest about wrong doing, repenting of it, and seeking forgiveness are things you can do in response to your guilt. To deal with your shame, you must actually be different . . . being vulnerable is not easy, especially when you have been hurt.[5]*

I *highly* commend the book from which this quote originated, *Overcoming Shame: Let Go of Others' Expectations and Embrace God's Acceptance* by Dr. Mark W. Baker, for more insight into this vital area of understanding. Mark led me on a path of discovery that connected the dots to my upbringing and family of origin, my successes and failures, and the period of wandering, all of which God used to draw me closer to him.

We return to the source of wisdom on the foolishness—in fact, the destructiveness—of living a life that attempts to surreptitiously hide from God.

> *The heart is deceitful above all things and beyond cure. Who can understand it? I the LORD search the heart and examine the mind, to reward a man according to his conduct, according to what his deeds deserve.* (**Jer. 17:9–10**)

> *There is nothing concealed that will not be disclosed, or hidden that will not be made known.* (**Matt. 10:26**)

> *Judge nothing before the appointed time, wait until the Lord comes. He will bring to light what is hidden in darkness and will expose the matters of the heart.* (**1 Cor. 4:5**)

> *There is nothing concealed that will not be disclosed, or hidden that will not be made known. What you have said in the dark will be heard in the daylight, and what you have whispered in the ear in the inner rooms will be proclaimed from the roofs.* (**Luke 12:2–3**)

So many of us have come to think of our Holy God, omniscient, omnipresent, and omnipotent, as some kind of benign friend to whom we can drag our daily pettiness and petitions. We need to repent, and work out our salvation in fear and trembling.

> *Now all has been heard; here is the conclusion of the matter:*
> *Fear God and keep his commandments, for this is the*
> *duty of all mankind. For God will bring every deed into*
> *judgement, including every hidden thing, whether it is good*
> *or evil.* **(Eccl. 12:13–14)**

Chapter 12
GRACE AND MERCY

God's mercy and grace give me hope—for myself and for our world. — **Billy Graham**

$\mathcal{I}$ was a twenty-two-year old student leader who had just completed my college degree, guiding our group of six on a two-month-long mission trip to India. Our train was by no means express. We had already stopped a mind-numbing amount of times on our 200-kilometer journey from Delhi to Saharanpur. Chai wallahs regularly hawked their tea, offered in communal cups which they filled repeatedly for each thirsty customer. We were headed to the Himalayan foothills in the far northwest corner of Uttar Pradesh State, bordering Nepal and China. Our final destination was Mussoorie, about 6,600 feet in elevation. Our plan included an additional visit to Dehradun in adjacent Uttarakhand State.

In the middle of the night I woke up coughing and hacking as thick smoke filled my lungs. I had been sleeping on the top tier of three pull-down planks, masquerading as bunk beds, on both sides of a narrow cubicle on this northbound train; our budget only allowed for a third-class ticket. The windows were open and bright orange flames licked our rail car. Even at this evening hour, besides the fire, the temperature outside was around 38°C.

The repetitive sound of the train wheels turning started to slow and we heard a lot of shouting. Still groggy, we grabbed our large backpacks that contained everything we brought and followed the stream of passengers down the rusty stairs, once the train came to a complete stop. On this journey our hosts were meeting us, not accompanying us, and English speakers were not common on third-class trains.

Once outside with the bugs and humidity, we watched and waited, unable to understand the full scope of our situation. Apparently, red-hot flying embers from this WP-class locomotive, running on high-ash Indian coal, had caught on fire two cars up from us; we were the third in line. The engineer's helpers decoupled the three burning cars and separated them from both the front and rear cars. Hundreds of people waited in the scrub and grass on both sides of the train—women in their colorful sarees, men in their white dhotis, many children, others bent with age and infirmity, plus six soot-faced Americans. Where was an enterprising chai wallah when you needed one?

For five hours we waited while the fire burned itself out. It started to rain like a hot, sticky shower. The engine eventually coupled the front portion of the train and pulled it to our destination. When it returned, it pulled the three burnt hulks of rail cars to somewhere, which took less time. Finally, it returned to recouple with our rear cars of the train to bring us to Saharanpur.

We arrived at our intermediary destination late, dirty, tired, and disoriented. Disembarking was unlike anywhere in the world. We had been warned earlier to get our belongings and stand by the open doors while the train was still slowing. Then at the first opportunity, *before* the train came to a full stop, we were to push out aggressively while the embarking passengers pushed in frantically. Somehow, we all made it in one piece.

Beggars and baggage handlers accosted us immediately. We were saved by our hosts who flagged us down. They had hired two small, non-airconditioned taxis. We crammed in with our gear at our feet and on our laps, for the upwardly winding and exhausting three-hour ride.

Three-quarters of the journey was not on paved roads. Upon arrival at the mission compound, we gratefully accepted our modest dormitory bunking. It included a simple washing facility where we scooped water from a six-inch ladle out of a large metal tub intended to last us many days. The tandoori chicken and rice tasted like a king's feast after our journey. We all fell exhausted, into a deep sleep. A few of us woke up during the night while rats scurried below our metal-framed beds.

That morning we realized that thousands of rambunctious lemur monkeys made their home here. Every important visit, meeting, and travel in between gave opportunity for these impertinent primates to interrupt us constantly. They were better pickpockets than the professionals in Mumbai! On one of our walks up the steep mountain roads we passed a snake man, who for the requested number of rupees, let me put his nine-foot python around my neck and shoulders for a good photo.

This exotic place was just 245 miles from beautiful Kashmir, current site of intense border hostilities between Indian and Chinese army units. Just 120 miles further to the west was Islamabad, today a cauldron of Islamist threats against the Christian community as well as the Pakistani government. Our visit included speaking in churches and small home gatherings, visiting with the expatriate missionaries to learn and observe, and to bring a smile and a touch of God's love to many children.

Python, Mussoorie, India

You may ask what eternal value could a band of traveling students have on India, or anywhere? I can affirm now, looking back years later, the evidence of God's grace and mercy from this humble beginning. On this particular trip we had already visited the Taj Mahal in Agra, the Red Fort in Dehli, and all the way to the southernmost tip of India, Cape Comorin, now called Kanyakumari in Tamil Nadu State. But our primary purpose was to support our colleague Mathews Chacko. He and his wife Rachel were returning from a period of residence and work in the US. They were praying deeply about how they should serve the people of their homeland. We joined them and their local leaders, looking for land to build a new school. Today, Bethany Academy in Tiruvalla, Kerala State is a highly respected institution, graduating emerging Christian leaders in a time of aggressive Hindu nationalism. They also fund a Power Vision TV network which beams the good news of Christ to most corners of this hungry land of 1.4 billion people. Some are hungry for food; many others *are* hungry for spiritual direction.

There is no question that Mother Teresa's "Home of the Pure Heart" (*Nirmal Hriday*), previously called Home for the Dying Destitutes, in Kalighat, Kolkata (Calcutta) is a powerful expression of God's grace and mercy. As I approached her facility walking on Anami

Mother Teresa's Home for the Dying Destitutes

Sangha (street) I passed the Kalighat Kali Temple dedicated to Kali, the Hindu goddess of time and change. Unsyncopated music was blaring, accentuated by crescendos of clashing symbols. Scattered garbage and rotting fruit skins did not deter the hyperactive crowds who jostled with the many vendors selling freshly strung flower garlands and a host of religious artifacts. Scrawny dogs and half-dressed kids ran across my path.

As I approached the entrance, a sleeping, comatose, or possibly dead human was scrunched into the gutter. It was impossible to determine gender, as this ultra-thin person was wrapped completely from head to toe with a sheer muslin cloth. Because of an old wall, the contour of the curb, and the direction of the entrance walkway, I had to step over this person to reach the men's ward.

When I went past the entrance and was ushered into the main area, a blessed quiet hit me. The room was dimly lit, with gently circulating fans providing a refreshing coolness. Beds with sleeping bodies on their gentle blue coverings filled the space. I cannot fully describe it, but there was a holiness to the place. Embracing the dignity of all human life Mother Teresa said, when she established this peaceful respite, "A beautiful death is for people who lived like animals to die like angels, loved and wanted."[1] This visit enlivened and empowered my understanding of what I would do, to encourage those in my sphere of influence. Over many years we have provided material aid and spiritual encouragement to this land of great need that God loves dearly.

Twenty years later, again visiting Dehradun, this time with Dr. Jack and a group of supporters, we stayed with my friend and fellow Fuller Seminary alumni Rev. Dr. George *and* Leela Chavanikamannil, who with God's calling and provision had started the Luther W. New Jr. Theological College. They have been training vibrant and bold Christian leaders, to speak the truth in an environment increasingly hostile to the gospel. If you are reading this book *and* perhaps seeking a place that makes a difference for the kingdom, this ministry and the one previously described are worth your investment.

Consistent with our strong global focus on serving Christian health institutions, we visited and later supported with medical equipment and supplies Herbertpur Christian Hospital, the Emmanuel

Hospital Association, and Landour Community Hospital. We also supplied many small church-based health and pharmacy depots. Another very worthwhile organization is Rev. Victor Paul Ministries in Chennai (formerly Madras). Their Christian schools bring young people into faith and develop them into productive citizens. Victor has been a blessing to many.

Pastor Victor's church, Chennai

It was time for Dr. Jack and I to travel on to Nepal. We said a fond farewell to our faithful accompanying donors, ending our time with a closing prayer for God's traveling *mercies* to go before them and us.

The seven-hour train ride back to Dehli was less harrowing than the train I had taken twenty years earlier. The flight to Kathmandu on Royal Nepal Air Carriers (now Nepal Airlines) was uneventful. I reflected in my journal: *I cannot describe the filth, the poverty, the heat, the sewage, the insanity, the hopelessness of much of India. Yet by the Lord's grace he is shedding light and truth to those in need with indigenous leaders being raised up. Looking around at the passengers on this flight, there are more westerners and weirdos than normal.*

Experienced global travelers know that the Thamel (tourist) District of Kathmandu is *the* place to freely buy almost anything—hashish, cannabis, opium, heroin, and other hard drugs. It was for sure, in that day, a hippie hangout. No hippies today, just pseudo-enlightened postmodern wanderers—still lost. Drugs are illegal today throughout Nepal, but Kathmandu remains the motherload of availability, especially during Shivaratri festival. Keep in mind that their neighbors are the Golden Crescent countries of Afghanistan, Pakistan, and Iran; these three countries alone supply much of the world's illegal substances that kill us—along with the synthetic stuff like fentanyl that comes from China. In fact, today underground labs in China are devising potent new opiates faster than authorities can respond.

As I sat back in my seat and rested fitfully, I recalled some of my earlier experiences. On one trip to India we stayed in a real fleabag "hotel." This negative-one rated facility had beads instead of doors, with drugged-out travelers each splayed out on dirty mattresses on the floor. The squat hole in lieu of a toilet, with porcelain "Frankenstein feet" to guide one's squatting, dropped each person's business *directly* from the fourth floor to the third and so on, down to the basement. Pity the persons who happened "to go" at the same time!

When we landed, we were graciously received by our hosts with TEAM.[2] We stayed at a simple but comfortable guest house. A shower, good meal, and decent night's sleep can do wonders. It was just past monsoon season so the clouds still covered the snow-graced peaks. We did a quick tour of some places of interest including the Himalayan Club and the famous Monkey Temple.[3]

Knowing the complexities of the process, our hosts arranged our booking on the twin-prop De Havilland operated by Necon Air. This route made a once-per-week run to a grass landing strip in the heart of the picturesque Chaur Jahari Valley. Our purpose for traveling to this remote, central Nepal region was to see how we could assist TEAM in equipping a small hospital they were building there. I settled into the late afternoon flight with the English language *Kathmandu Post* and some rumbling in my intestines. We landed with a welcoming party of five from the McKinney family and a few lookers-on. Baggage claim was "pick it up yourself at the tail of the plane." The three children of Dr. Ted and Rachel McKinney were cute, lively, and inquisitive. We took a liking to them all instantly.

As darkness approached, we noticed there were no lights and were advised that they came on for two hours only, *most nights*, from around sixish to eightish. There was a lot of "ish" stuff in this remote place; not much was predictable. We shared a meal of fresh applesauce, a cucumber salad, and homemade pizza. We were joined by the TEAM engineer Dave, wife Ann, and a young woman teaching English for the Peace Corps in a remote village outside Nepal Gunj. In her daily existence there was *no* electricity or running water.

With great animation the stories began to unfold. We listened to them talk about the work they currently did at the Living Waters Health Clinic and what kinds of health interventions were most common: people with lots of pus, pain, and fevers; malaria; lice; gastrointestinal issues; and snake bites. Just the day before we arrived Dr. McKinney said they had caught and killed three cobras in our outhouse. Yikes! We learned of their plans and hopes for the future. And once the lights clicked off in this small village, we talked by candlelight for another hour about faith, family, and mutual connections. When it was time to move to our sleeping quarters, we looked up at the night sky which was absolutely stunning—a tapestry of millions of sparkling diamonds on a celestial sheet of black velvet. As we drifted off to sleep, we were serenaded to sleep by crickets, peepers, and other interesting night noises.

Our first morning, we awoke to roosters and the tinkling bells of passing donkeys. My journal explained: *We are on the most ancient trade route between China and India where they traded spices, silk, tea, porcelain, and other goods for millennia.* During our visit we did a lot of stumbling in the dark, made a lot of trips per day with diarrhea to the outhouse (no cobras!), and took splendid walks into the foothills. We *did* accomplish our mission, making a specific plan and timetable to support this important medical outpost whose "ministry of presence" and health care were delivered by a dedicated band of believers. By the time our once-per-week flight arrived—which for two days we were advised might not make it until next week—we were ready to go home!

Grace and mercy are inherent in the nature of God. Love and peace are also. How does this apply to his relationship to humankind? Again, we turn to Scripture, since all we know of God is what he has revealed to us in his Word:

> *Let us then approach God's throne of grace with confidence, so that we may receive mercy and find grace to help us in our time of need.* (**Heb. 4:16**)
>
> *Grace, mercy, and peace from God the Father and Christ Jesus our Lord.* (**1 Tim. 1:2**)
>
> *But to each one of us grace has been given as Christ apportioned it.* (**Eph. 4:7**)
>
> *Grace and peace be yours in abundance through the knowledge of God and of Jesus our Lord.* (**2 Pet. 1:2**)
>
> *Mercy, peace, and love be yours in abundance.* (**Jude 2**)
>
> *Have mercy on me, O God, according to your unfailing love; according to your great compassion blot out my transgressions. Wash away all my iniquity and cleanse me from my sin.* (**Ps. 51:1–2**)

In the writing style of that day, hand-scribed letters began with identifying who was speaking; then addressed their audience; then included some expression of affection, blessing, or good will preceding the main content of the letter. Clearly, grace and mercy—peace and love—are used often. Were these just intended as polite salutations? No. They were, in fact, acknowledged expressions of the nature of God toward his people, meant to bless and encourage.

Translating the common Greek of that New Testament era, χάρις is the noun form of "grace." Its essential meaning is unmerited favor, with a clear connection to the divine influence upon the heart. The earlier passages cited give us insight. The place where God abides, his throne, is full of grace. Grace is something good which God wants to give us in abundance. And grace is a blessing that each of the writers of Scripture desire for us to have more of. Possessing this gift of grace brings us peace and a sense of being loved.

The noun form of the Greek for "mercy" is ἔλεος. This word expresses pity resulting in forgiveness, with a clear connection to love that responds to human need. God understands that we are dust—that we now exist in an estranged relationship with him. We are lost and need to be reconnected with our Creator. There are, of course, other root words, tenses, and derivatives of meaning. This is just a simple explanation.

God has chosen to establish his kingdom, to accomplish his will and purpose *in relationship*, in partnership with us. Jesus modeled grace and mercy. It is both a biblical mandate and our privilege to extend grace, and sometimes mercy, to those around us. Our Lord will certainly use us in this way toward our spouse, our child, a neighbor, or work associate. Where it gets especially hard is when we feel in our gut, know in our spirit, that we *need* to extend grace (blessing) or mercy (forgiveness) to someone who humiliated us, slandered us, hurt us, or even abused us! I still wrestle with that portion of the Lord's Prayer that says, "Forgive us the wrongs we have done, as we forgive the wrongs that others have done to us" (Matt. 6:12, GNT)

One of the most impactful examples of grace and mercy, for me personally, involves *New York Times* best-selling author Ron Hall. His book (and later major motion picture) *Same Kind of Different as Me* describe, "A dangerous homeless drifter who grew up picking cotton in virtual slavery. An upscale art dealer accustomed to the world of Armani and Chanel. A gutsy woman with a stubborn dream. A story so incredible no novelist would dare to dream it."[4] One endorser wrote, "*Same Kind of Different as Me* is a compelling story of tragedy, triumph, perseverance, dedication, faith and the resilience of the human spirit." I won't spoil the book or movie—buy it and watch it!

I was privileged to meet Ron at a reception held in the lovely Beverly McNeil Gallery[5] in Birmingham, Alabama. John and Beverly McNeil were hosting this function preceding a major fundraiser the following day at The Club, where Ron was speaking on behalf of The Lovelady Center.[6] This Holy Spirit-inspired rehabilitation program serves around five hundred formerly addicted, abused, and incarcerated women, *and* those with children. Founded by Brenda Lovelady Spahn, it is now capably managed by her daughter Melinda Megahee, with other family members shouldering the load. It is a place of irrefutable grace and mercy!

Since I had served the homeless in Skid Row Los Angeles for five years, I had some understanding of Ron's experience with what became the New Beginnings Mission in the "across the tracks" part of Dallas. Here, many people with dark challenges and overwhelming odds were served. Ron's wife Deborah was the catalyst whom God used for much redemptive change in his life as well as the mission's clients. We chatted and exchanged mutual experiences. I identified with many of his discoveries, *especially* when he said, "Looking back now, I mourn the mutual wounds inflicted in verbal battles with the 'unsaved.' In fact, I have chosen to delete that particular term from my vocabulary as I have learned that even with my $500 European-designer bifocals, I cannot see into a person's heart to know his spiritual condition. All I can do is tell the jagged tale of my own spiritual journey and declare that my life has been the better for having followed Christ."

Ron's presentation at the gala attended by seven hundred people followed the truly inspiring music of Charles Billingsley. When he sang the Lord's Prayer a capella there was a hushed reverence. Following Ron's inspiring talk, a line of about twenty "Loveladies" cued to step up to the raised platform as Charles sang "Bridge over Troubled Water." One woman at a time walked up and over, first holding one side of their 20 x 30 inch posterboard to the audience, then flipping it around midway across:

- I was addicted to opiates for a decade . . . BUT now I have been clean for eighteen months.
- I was pimped and sex trafficked since I was fifteen years old . . . BUT now I am training to be a dental tech.
- I was in prison for seven years . . . BUT now I am free in Christ Jesus.
- My partner beat me severely and tried to kill me . . . BUT now I am a counselor in our trauma department.
- I had lost my three kids to the state child protection service . . . BUT now they are home and they love me again.

Everyone at our table of ten, including a movie producer, business owners, and a senior pastor—and as far as I could tell, most everyone at the other sixty-nine tables—had tears running down their faces. I believe this will be *our* reaction when *we* find ourselves on the other side of our mortality and time on earth. Filled with overwhelming gratitude for God's grace and mercy, he will show us, on the day of judgment and life review how *we* lived it. It wasn't all pretty, but Jesus paid the price. "Truly I tell you, whatever you did for one of the least of these brothers and sisters of mine, you did for me" (Matt. 25:40).

Grace does not choose a man and leave him as he is.
— **Charles Spurgeon**

Chapter 13
FORGIVENESS AND HEALING

I think that if God forgives us, we must forgive ourselves. — **C. S. Lewis**

As I shared earlier, my battle to forgive—to release a grievance and let God deal with it—is a struggle I am making headway with. I had a tendency—no, a propensity—to keep accounts and remember wrongs that had been done to me. Subliminally, I would look for a time and opportunity to even the score. Thankful I have made significant progress, considering this is completely contrary to God's sanctifying purposes: "Do not take revenge, my dear friends, but leave room for God's wrath, for it is written: 'It is mine to avenge; I will repay, says the Lord.'. . . Do not be overcome by evil, but overcome evil with good" (Rom. 12:19, 21). Each of us has our areas of spiritual vulnerability. My struggle with impatience and forgiveness is a constant battle. I fully expect to be wrestling with these challenges until I cross into eternity. Nonetheless, God has been steadily removing the dross with his refining fire.

After my divorce was legally final, I relocated and leased a condo with a 180-degree view of the Pacific Ocean. It was one element in my effort to *start again*. In this period, I did a lot of reflecting, writing, and journaling, many times watching an awesome sunset sitting on my balcony. San Diego County has some of the best weather in America, so it was possible to do this virtually year-round.

As part of my healing process, I joined an instructive twelve-week long program focused on men—and more importantly, taught by men who had been through their own challenges. The course included topics that *we* men universally wrestle with. Every Tuesday night a large group of us met for a plenary teaching session, then broke into smaller groups for discussion and prayer. I found the entire exercise redemptive and valuable. To varying degrees, I had some level of affinity for and an understanding of each topic. Yet, during discussion times I often found myself functioning more like a facilitator than a participant.

When weeks ten and eleven rolled around that dynamic changed completely. The two topics were forgiveness and bitterness. When forgiveness for a wrong done is not dealt with, when it remains in our heart, bitterness takes root with destructive consequences. In my syllabus I underlined or highlighted *something* on every page with marginal notes going in all directions. Clearly this topic resonated with my life journey. I'd like to share elements from this curriculum,[1] and also draw living water from the well of true wisdom, Holy Scripture.

When the disciples asked Jesus to teach **us** how to pray—his model, his template, his instruction included, "Forgive our sins, for we also forgive everyone who sins against us" (Luke 11:4). There are two distinct elements here. First, we need to ask God to forgive *our* sins, on a regular basis. Jesus instructed us, "when you pray, say . . ." (Luke 11:2). Second, there is both an acknowledgement and a mandate from Jesus, that we need to forgive all who sin *against us*. And not just seven times but as many times as needed, *and* for as long as it takes! We may not lose our salvation for *not* fully forgiving everyone in our life who hurt us, but if we don't there are damaging effects. Forgiveness is for *our* benefit. Holding on to a grievance is like drinking poison and hoping the other guy dies. Lack of forgiveness *always* hurts us and keeps us in bondage. Without forgiveness the poison grows into something that changes us. Keep in mind, I am speaking as a wounded healer.[2]

There is a rock-solid benchmark laid out in God's Word. "For *if* you forgive other people when they sin against you, your heavenly Father *will also* forgive you. But, *if* you do not forgive others their sins, your Father *will not* forgive your sins" (Matt. 6:14–15, emphasis added). "Forgiveness is *the crown jewel of love*. It is the second most precious gift for the human soul, behind the gift of salvation. The Father's supreme gift to humanity was forgiveness through the sacrificial death and resurrection of his Son. The only door to eternal life *and emotional freedom* is through forgiveness. If we do not forgive one another we remain in bondage—to anger, to resentment, to bitterness and, many times, to actual physical illness. We can prohibit the fullness of God's grace in our lives if we withhold forgiveness."[3] It is often said that the highest form of worship is obedience. Thus, to forgive is the supreme test of obedience. How interesting that most of us will trust a doctor, presuming she or he is well trained. When they order a surgery, which will involve the cutting away of part of our body, we allow it. We believe it will ultimately contribute to our health and well-being. How much more should we embrace God's guidance regarding forgiveness.

During this period, I decided to learn as much as I could about forgiveness, and what I *must* do to apply it. This *was* my goal and it *is* the path I am still pursuing. *But* there's this Korean attorney who slandered me . . . and I . . . well, I'm still working on it!

Forgiveness begins with fully acknowledging that an injustice was done to you. It wasn't fair. You didn't deserve it. It hurts. It could be neglect or abuse, an unexpected betrayal or a careless word spoken with insensitivity, or perhaps something of value stolen. Forgiveness is hard, it doesn't come easy, and it will take time. "Forgiveness is not saying it didn't matter; it is not saying we simply choose to overlook the offense. Forgiveness is saying the Cross is enough . . . forgiveness is releasing the person to God for him to deal with."[4] Forgiveness also requires a season of protest, a period of anger, a time of grief. Most of all, forgiveness is for *our* healing. To give up our choice to take revenge allows mercy to triumph over judgment. It is not possible to fully reach a place of forgiveness until we have dealt with the emotional trauma of the injustice.

Ignoring it is not an option. If we try to ignore our hurt, the alternative is growing bitterness. Out of this, we experience resentment, shame, and sometimes obsessive or destructive thoughts. What we don't always realize, as we focus on the person who hurt us, is that at the center of our struggle is spiritual warfare, which our enemy wages against us mercilessly.

As I sat on my third-story balcony, overlooking an azure blue ocean, I started on my homework:

1. I have had trouble forgetting the following injustices . . .

2. I have had trouble forgiving the following people . . .

3. The situations that have made it difficult for me to forgive are . . .

4. By holding a grudge, what do I hope to accomplish?

5. How has resentment worked for me?[5]

In a relatively short span of time I had filled multiple pages with responses. Astoundingly, for question #2 my list included twenty people—which I added to later! I organized each set of rough notes then determined that it was time to schedule my annual (and sometimes semi-annual) two-night, three-day retreat. Over the years I have sought respite in some beautiful, peaceful places where physical seclusion enhances spiritual intimacy. Of special significance to me is my time of quiet reflection at St. Andrew's Abbey, a Benedictine community in the high desert town of Valyermo, California. When I returned from this time of refreshment, I had consolidated a typed document which helped me specifically focus during my daily prayer time:

> *Father . . . heal, release, remove . . . the hurt, anger, pain . . . from my heart, mind, spirit FOR [and then I listed a series of bullet-points of those events and people that I allowed to stay unforgiven]—until now.*

We have focused on the need to forgive others—including God. An important topic, but one we have insufficient space and time to address here, is *forgiving ourselves.* There are volumes written on this vital spiritual exercise. We all fall short. We all screw up sometimes. We all regret that we hurt _____. We tell ourselves in our private thoughts, if *only* I had not done _____. If only I could turn back the hands of time. This bridge of healing, to forgive yourself, is one you *can* cross, if you put your mind, heart and will to the task. In the words of Leo Buscaglia, "Love yourself. Accept yourself. Forgive yourself, because without you the rest of us are without a source of many wonderful things."[6]

The final area of forgiveness I wish to briefly consider is the need to forgive the collective sins, oppression, injustice of a nation, political system, or culture. Holy moly, can you really cover this topic adequately? Of course *not*, but we must briefly address it. Let's begin with my travel reflections to Cuba, via Mexico City and Nicaragua.

As a Christian CEO of a charitable organization I had unique invitations and opportunities to travel in countries that are either restricted or not on the main routes of normal tourist traffic; the preceding chapters already validate this. On this occasion I was traveling to Havana, Cuba with an invitation from the Concilio Ecuménico de Iglesias (Ecumenical Council of Churches). This particular visit went through Mexico City to first attend the annual conference for the Association of Evangelical Relief & Development Organizations (now called the ACCORD Network). At a future date I was elected for a three-year rotation as this organization's president, a collateral duty to my main responsibilities. Our host was the excellent organization AMEXTRA[7] working with the poorest of the poor throughout Mexico. For more than thirty-five years they have provided health, nutrition, education, resource generation, and other services. Beyond our meetings, presentations, and future plans we all immersed ourselves in the reality of their ministry.

Along with four young people dressed in clown suits, we piled into two ten passenger vans. Our goal was to brighten the hearts and feed the stomachs of the children who lived in the infamous "Neza Garbage Dump." This was located in Nezahualcóyotl, a poor outlying area of the megapolis of Mexico City, with a population of twenty-two million. Many hundreds of people made their home and living scavenging for items, seven days a week, to either use themselves or recycle for a few pesos. Criminal overseers always extract a cut. Convoys of trucks drop 1,200 tons of garbage a day in this seventy-four-acre mountain of misery. Once pilfered, the refuse is either bulldozed into compost or burned. This land area was reclaimed after Lake Texcoco was drained, creating more space for the burgeoning population. The mud from recent rains, the smells, and the noise are impossible to adequately describe here.

At one intersection of two muddy roads our team set up speakers and started to play lively Christian music, *en español* of course. Old carpets were laid out for the gathering children to sit on. Volunteers were simultaneously going into all the plastic shanties and cardboard shacks, handing out fliers. The amazing thing about the four clowns is that *each* of them had found the Lord in this very place! They were now ambassadors for Christ in their neighborhood. God redeems, then intentionally uses *us* as his channels of mercy.

As they began their lighthearted program more and more kids streamed in. With passion and empathy, there were now more than one hundred kids eagerly engaged in action songs, memorizing a few Scripture verses, watching mime displays and playing games. Eventually the cover over the big cooking pot of lentil soup was opened, and workers filled plastic bowls handed out with a generous hunk of fresh bread. Each child eagerly devoured it. After a prayer of benediction, they all scattered back to their scavenging.

We left with burning throats from the toxic fumes that permeated this city of desperation. But our hearts were transformed with the understanding that when we serve the least of these we are, in fact, serving and honoring our Lord.

With required visas in hand, faxed to the airline desk agent in Mexico City literally minutes before they shut the doors without us, we boarded our one-stop flight to Havana. After clearing the bureaucratic formalities at José Martí International Airport, we were greeted by Pastors David, José, and Ontoniel (I will not use family names). We checked into the Hotel Habana Libre, formerly the Hilton, but nowhere close in comparable amenities or service from its heyday. At one time Havana was one of the hottest tickets in the Caribbean for night life and raucous fun. Everything in this country seemed to be frozen in time, not the least of which were legions of cars from the 1950s, held together by the most innovative means.

The 26th of July Movement established communist rule under Fidel Castro, and since 1965 this island nation has been under this government. The purpose of our first trip was to build relationships, assess needs,

Typical old car, Havana

and determine the best way to work through the challenges of sending humanitarian aid into an environment of embargos and political complexities.

The medical portion of the week-long visit included meetings with the Ministries of Health and Religious Affairs as well as the Medical Commission for the Ecumenical Council. Specific permissions were granted, then an itinerary planned for "official" visits to Aballí Pediatric Hospital, Miguel Rodriguez Hospital, El Hospital Hijas de Galicia (daughters of grace), the February 24th Home for the Aged, Hospital Iluminado, and various polyclinics. The level of training of the Cuban medical community is quite advanced. In fact, for decades Cuban doctors have filled vacancies in places like Venezuela (where they still serve), Angola, and other so-called nonaligned countries—translation: where there is a geopolitical value for doing so.

With little doubt, our trip was also approved to take place at a time of high celebration for the anniversary of Havana and the landing of Christopher Columbus. Nobody tearing down statues of ole Christopher C. here! Thus, we were given preferred seating for some great performances of salsa and swing dance, with their distinct Afro-Caribbean tempo, including Guaguanco and Pachanga. We enjoyed super-talented singers including Latin pop and opera. And there were choirs of patriotic citizens and lots of flags. Since most dinners don't start until 10 p.m. in Havana, we made it back in time for our leisurely evening on the twenty-fifth floor of the Cabaret Turquin.

In the course of our Havana days we *did* visit many places of historic interest. We purchased a few items, which could only be secured with US dollars, at the formerly fashionable Miramar District. A box of twenty-five Cohibas, even then, cost $285 George Ws. Miramar was certainly fashionable in the days when Ernest Hemingway hung out here. We ate at the historic Hotel Nacional de Cuba, vacation stop and celebrity magnet for people like Marlon Brando, Frank Sinatra,

Elizabeth Taylor, and more than a few New York and Chicago mafia dons. But today it still draws the likes of Beyonce and JZ, Rihanna, Mick Jagger, and Katy Perry. Here pools, peacocks, piña coladas, and La Cervezas Cristal were in abundance. The surrounding district is filled with loud clubs and bars, with predictable Cuban attire—bright and tight. During the zenith of this city of the night it was said, "Havana is a mistress of pleasure, the lush and opulent goddess of delights." My journal captured a brief image: *This place is crawling with illicit activity.*

We also enjoyed Old Havana with its historic Fortress of San Carlos de la Cabaña and the Port of Havana, fortified by the Spanish in 1553. On selected nights, the impressive canons are ignited at 9 p.m. During the height of Cuba's independent history there were sixty-four artillery pieces protecting this port of entry. Some historic battles were fought here, including the two-month siege by the British in 1762 and the sinking of the US warship *Maine* in 1898 which touched off the Spanish-American War.

We shared meals a few times at a private *paladar*, our favorite Rancho Verde. These eating establishments, sometimes in outdoor settings, are operated by individual families at their homes. Typical fare was black beans and rice, with chicken when it was available, and plantain chips (dried banana). Thankfully, the government eventually allowed private enterprise to generate some hard currency and to take *some* of the bite out of their suffocatingly restrictive coupon-rationing system. Traveling with our dear pastors we learned about their restrictions. First, they could only shop on two days of the week. There was a paucity of selection. My journal explains further: *No liters of gas available for three months when paying in Cuban pesos; a quarter pound of meat every nine days; milk only available for children one to seven years old; one-and-a-half bars of soap per month; two ounces of coffee every fifteen days.*

After completing our official visits, it was a blessing and privilege to spend private time with our host pastors. They represented multiple denominations (Reformed, Pentecostal, Methodist, Baptist), as well as house church leaders. With them we really experienced how *most* Cuban people live.

We packed a smaller traveling bag for our three-day visit to Matanzas Province southeast of Havana with our final stop Jaguey Grande, simply known as Jagüey. It was eye-opening to realize the lengths our hosts went through to prepare for us. Since we now understood how difficult it was for them to get gas and basic food supplies, I asked, "What can we do?"

They laughed and exclaimed with a smile, "*You* can get anything at the 'dollar store.'" So we did. I paid for and filled up the gas on two private cars. We bought what they said we needed for our travel. But I decided this alone was not sufficient and I purchased extra coffee, shampoo, toothpaste, and more. It's hard to express how overjoyed this simple gesture made them. One pastor's wife at our destination cried as she told us that our gift of coffee represented one year's ration!

On the way, we passed Bahía de Cochinos (Bay of Pigs, also the same word for Triggerfish) in the Gulf of Cazones in sight of Isla Cayo Romano. In 1961, under the direction of President Kennedy, who inherited this plan from outgoing President Eisenhower, 1,400 CIA trained Cuban exiles launched their ill-advised and unsuccessful invasion. We stopped at various small dwellings to drop off food, listen, learn, and pray. The poverty was stunning, not to mention the humidity, deluge of rain, buzzing mosquitos, and slithering crocodiles. A swamp creature's abode for sure.

Old man and grandson, Jagüey

But our fellowship and worship with the believers was a joy. In one "church," people squatted on bare logs on the dirt floor. I was asked to bring a message and spoke from Philippians 3:10–14: "Participating in his suffering, pressing on, forgetting what lies behind and straining to what lies ahead." *What in God's name did I truly understand about suffering?* At one stop we prayed for the sick including a blind woman, and one with two feet amputated. At another stop we learned that our donated medicines saved seven lives. Two dozen people had traveled *all day* just to thank us!

We learned that the churches were rapidly growing especially the house churches. Many young people attended. We were told that political opposition was more subtle, though widespread. This prompted a future invitation and subsequent visit, alone this time, to specifically author an investigative article for *World Christian* magazine on God's spirit moving in Cuba, especially through the growth of the house church movement.

The church is the bride of Christ, not an institution. The incongruity and injustice of the haves and the should-haves always discourages me. Over a seven-year period we supported these humble and loving people with multiple shipments of medicines, medical supplies, Christian literature, and other necessities. My concluding journal entry: *Vibrant culture and beauty here, abysmal run-down conditions, eating in tourist hotels while most in the country are barely hanging on, the state trying to control God will never work, we sat unhurried and talked for hours never missing TV or the internet, bread lines, unbelievable patience in adversity, Pastor Erelio's concluding thought, "Together we are like Nehemiah, building ministry together."*

Biding a fond farewell to our Christian brothers and sisters as well as my traveling companions from the US, I had one final stop in Nicaragua. This particular visit centered around a Rotary grant where Rotary One in Chicago matched a local chapter to fund a health project on Ometepe Island in the middle of Lake Nicaragua, the largest in Central America. It was formed by two active volcanoes, Volcán Concepción and Volcán Maderas. This beautiful ecotourist wonderland was inhabited during the Dinarte Phase (c 2000 BC-500 BC) by the Chorotega natives; we can glean some of their culture from the petroglyphs carved into the abundant basal rock. My small company, Global Med Partners, was providing two mobile diagnostic laboratories, which enabled the rapid diagnosis required for most primary health needs. Accurate and rapid diagnosis is critical for effective treatment. Many people live days away, by local transport, from a health facility with tertiary laboratory services. Access to our portable diagnostic units was invaluable for the local health practitioners.

We worked in partnership with the Fundación Totoco. The project was successful and greatly appreciated. We also sent a shipment of needed items to the Little Blue Bird Orphanage (*Parjarito Azul*) where eighty-five sweet kids were cared for. It is a home for physically and mentally impaired children. Since Bristol is my special-needs child, now in heaven, you can imagine my passion for this place.

On this visit I traveled with my dear friend Eglert Gutierrez, who had fled Cuba because of his newly found faith in Jesus. As a military officer and engineer, the government sent him to Moscow to get his master's degree. Someone in his position could not believe in God! Eglert was not imprisoned, but was fired and isolated. He started baking bread and rolls at home to survive. He eventually escaped in the dead of night. Today Eglert is a mechanical engineer in Palm Desert, California with Maria, his vibrant Christian partner.

Eglert had done business in Nicaragua, so he supplemented our short visit with a few trips to some mountain regions. I especially enjoyed Lake Masaya in the center of Masaya Volcano National Park. We drove into the picturesque coffee-producing highlands, with Matagalpa as a welcomed watering hole for lunch. Eglert knew that I enjoy a good cigar now and then, so we headed to Esteli where many cigar factories employed hundreds of women rolling, labeling, and boxing some of the best cigars outside of Cuba. At the Plascencia Factory I picked up a box of twenty for just $100. Returning to Managua we stopped at the Selva Negra, the Black Jungle. The mosquitos there rivaled any I had swatted in Africa, India, or Cuba!

Finally, I was on another trip home, long overdue. I returned with disruptive memories of more places of overwhelming need, while resonating with Bob Pierce, founder of World Vision, who once said, "Let my heart be broken with the things that break the heart of God."

What do *we* do when there is systemic injustice in the country we live in? Considering the current social movements underway in the US and around the world it is a timely topic. Most people of every race and class believe there should be fair and equal treatment of all races and classes. Nearly everyone embraces the goal of eliminating racism and injustice. It is the right thing to do. The discerning Christian, who has a proper understanding of the presence and purpose of Satan, knows our enemy kills, steals, and destroys. There is no truth in him. He is a liar. And so, in America and every country under his temporary domain, he has diabolically changed the narrative. Through lies, deception, and obfuscation the enemy creates chaos and destruction. He causes hatred and enmity between people. "If it doesn't change, tear it down" is *not* a principle of Scripture.

Is there injustice in every country on the planet? Indeed, there is. The higher path is forgiveness. You cannot prey on someone that you pray for. I'm quite certain there are *not* a lot of praying people in streets of anarchy. "We are most like beasts when we kill. We are most like men when we judge. We are most like God when we forgive."[8]

Something tells me I am not the only person who had a list of people to forgive, a list of hurts to let go of. "Jus' guessin" . . . somewhere on our journey, we need to stop and take account. Are we holding something against God? Does a person come to mind, immediately, whom we need to forgive? Have we forgiven *ourselves* for deeds we regret? Do we feel resentment toward any human institution like government or political system, our workplace, or even a church? Every one of these has likely caused us pain and suffering. To experience freedom, to experience restoration, to find healing and to live in peace, we must seek to forgive. It's hard. Life is hard. "A good man brings good things out of the good stored up in him, and an evil man brings evil things out of the evil stored up in him. But I tell you that everyone will have to give account on the day of judgment for every empty word they have spoken. For by your words you will be acquitted, and by your words you will be condemned" (Matt. 12:35–37).

Chapter 14
WHAT REALLY MATTERS

God brings us into deep water, not to drown us but to cleanse us. —***James H. Aughey***[1]

*I*t is not for me to say what should really matter *to you*. We were all made in God's image with the singular uniqueness of every fingerprint, voice pattern, or snowflake. Your individual experience and God's redemptive work in your life on earth will determine what matters most to you. What I *can* tell you is that *my* life journey took me through some deep waters—but also to majestic mountains, glorious meadows, and radiant sunsets. I can relate to the Barry Gibb song lyric that says, "If tears were diamonds, I'd be a rich man now." From personal experience and persistent observation, I now understand that God *always* uses the crucible experiences in our lives to draw us to himself. Then he expects us to walk with others who are on a similar journey. A journal entry, here at home (not traveling) anchors my thought: *A light of discovery. A discovery of enlightenment just occurred, and it was written plainly in Scripture all along. Suffering produces endurance—perseverance. It is necessary for our growth. Suffering, trials and failure allow God to mold us into who we were destined to become.*

Many months ago, I had a dream. Unlike some people, I don't often recall my dreams, and God is not usually present in them. This one was short, but vivid. I had a sense of his *presence*. He handed me a torch light, blazingly bright. It was not a standard flashlight. A door opened and I was directed out into the dark. Hearing nothing audible, somehow, I knew what I was supposed to do. Carefully and intentionally I continued to walk, coming upon deep pits of various sizes in the barren ground. It was dark everywhere—only blacks and greys, with no color.

When I directed the bright light downward, there were groups of people, silent lips moving, begging me with their eyes to help them out. The pits were too deep for them to naturally remove themselves. I was not capable of helping them all myself, but I indicated through pantomime that I would return and assured them silently that I understood and they could count on me.

For some period of time I walked slowly in all directions, discovering *many* other pits. The condition of all the people in them was haggard and desperate. I sensed each was hampered by different types of bondage, some deeply and inextricably. This dream felt like a 1920s silent film. Suddenly I was in another place, standing up in a search boat in the icy Atlantic. My torch light again shone into the darkness. I was in the *one lifeboat* that returned to look for survivors of the Titanic. Most were frozen stiff, their fate sealed. But I *knew*, still in silence, that it was my urgent task to find the few who remained alive, who could be saved. I woke up in a sweat, and prayed. Since then I have sought discernment on how God intends to use me to engage in this divine direction—to help set the captives free.

Ravensbrück Concentration Camp for women (*Frauenlager*), fifty miles north of Berlin, was in operation from 1939 to 1945. It served as a training base for some 3,500 female SS (Nazi paramilitary corps) supervisors who staffed it and thirty-four other satellite camps, many of them at military industrial plants. About fifty thousand women died at Ravensbrück from disease, starvation, overwork, and despair.

Some inmates were used in medical experiments. Killing techniques at Ravensbrück evolved over time. At first, prisoners were shot in the back. Later, women were transported to a T4 Program killing center or to Auschwitz for gassing. Prisoners at Ravensbrück were also killed by lethal injection and cremated in the nearby resort town of Fürstenberg.

One brave woman who made it through this hell on earth was Cornelia Arnolda "Corrie" ten Boom, the author of the book *The Hiding Place*, which later became a inspiring movie of the same name. She was a Dutch Christian watchmaker who, with her family, helped many Jews escape the Nazi Holocaust. Once caught, she joined them in the death camp. I had the privilege of knowing and loving Corrie through her full-time nurse, Ellen de Kroon, who married our campus chaplain "Brother Bob" (Robert) Stamps. As I thought about Corrie, my mind returned to the spirit-filled service at the Mostar (Bosnia) Evangelical Church where this branch of the persecuted church sang the theme song of *The Hiding Place*, followed by the Hallelujah Chorus. To see how God intricately weaves one life with another—one book, movie, or song with another—and uses *you and me* who, in all eternity, can only reach *one* particular person to accomplish his purposes, is just out-of-sight awesome!

It hit me like a lightning bolt that no matter what the enemy does to thwart God's plan, almighty God is sovereign and *will* prevail. Through the sacrificial life, death, and resurrection of our Lord Jesus Christ, his everlasting victory is ours as well. Corrie ten Boom's haunting quote brings great hope in our most severe trials: "There is no pit so deep, that God's love is not deeper still."

Let's lighten the mood just a bit! One of the things that really matters is to enjoy life, the unique one God has given *you,* for as much time as he has allotted. Every day is a gift. And as mentioned earlier, "The chief purpose (end) of man is to glorify God and enjoy him forever." We don't need to wait to get to heaven to enjoy him. His handiwork, his marvelous creation, is all around us.

I spent memorable time in many of the countries comprising the diverse and beautiful continent of South America—Brazil, Peru, Colombia, Bolivia, Ecuador, Chile, and Argentina. Of course, we were always seeking opportunities to invest our energy and resources into ministries of compassion and mercy to the poor and needy. I will spare giving you another list of hospitals, clinics, and children's programs we visited and supported. Let me describe just two special places, with this thought: for those of you with the time and resources to do so, I highly recommend you visit Argentina and Chile, particularly their southern regions. I'm not sure why, but the Southern Hemisphere appeals to me in a unique way. What follows are a just few travel highlights, before ending this chapter and this book with what really matters . . . to me.

In Argentina you must visit the capital Buenos Aires, the cultural and culinary center of this magnificent country which spans 2,175 miles. On the western side is Villa La Angostura, an oasis of tranquility among the rugged mountains of Patagonia. Patagonia shares the massive Andes Mountains with neighboring Chile, serving as their de facto border; good luck trying to finding the legal demarcation line in much of this region.

In Argentina you can find steppes, grasslands, deserts, fjords, and temperate rainforests. Torres del Paine National Park, also in Patagonia, is known for its granite towers, icebergs, and the massive Grey Glacier.

Ushuaia is an Argentine port with

Torres del Paine, Patagonia   the Martial Mountains, scenic railway, plus access to Antarctica's penguins and skiing. The stunning Iguazú Falls lie along Argentina's border with Brazil, with Iguazú National Park on the Argentinian side and Iguaçu National Park on the Brazilian side. Another worthwhile place to visit is Patagonia's Los Glaciares National Park. Here the small town of El Calafate offers many quaint accommodations and other amenities. In the summer, Mar del Plata Beach comes alive with tourists. You can visit the Punta Mogotes, and Playa Grande is a surfer's delight. There is so much more to see and do!

In Chile, I love Santiago and Valparaíso equally. Renting a car for the scenic drive from Viña del Mar is well worth it. While you're at it, keep going all the way south to Puerto Montt at the northern end of the Reloncaví Sound. The alluring Lakes District, as this region is known, has some of the most unbelievably beautiful places to commune with the God who created them! Let me just rattle off a travel agent's list: Frutillar, Cochamo Valley, Villarrica. Vicente Perez Rosales National Park, Temuco, Puyehue National Park, and Valdivia. Of course, here as in Argentina, you can bundle up in *really* warm clothes and see all the glaciers that meet your heart's desire. Parque Nacional Laguna San Rafael is the best place to go. Chile spans 2,653 miles with an extremely diverse geography and seven different climate subtypes ranging from low desert in the north, to alpine tundra and glaciers south, and tropical rainforest on Easter Island. Rapa Nui, as this island is known by its earliest inhabitants, contains nine hundred giant stone statues, centuries old, with evidence of Polynesian cultural origins. Words alone are inadequate to describe this exotic part of the world.

Every road I have taken, physically and spiritually, over many years and many more miles, included the presence of the Lord. He was always there. Sometimes I leaned into his loving arms. Other times I hurried along, intense and unaware. But on this forty-year journey, I *did* discover what matters most to me. And these lessons conclude my story.

INVERTED WISDOM

"'For my thoughts are not your thoughts, neither are your ways my ways,' declares the LORD. 'As the heavens are higher than the earth, so are my ways higher than your ways and my thoughts than your thoughts'" (Isa. 55:8–9). We have already considered the eternal difference between knowledge and wisdom. When we study Scripture there are innumerable examples of how opposite our thoughts are to what God expects. In my own life journey, so much of what I thought was right was not wrong, but it was *less* than what God wanted for me. Some people need a fire lit under them to get moving. For me, God most often held on to my shirttail with a nudge to sit down and talk with him first.

God graciously placed these truths and safely pressed them between the pages in my heart:

- We believe strength means exercising power, dominance, and higher ability. But the Lord tells us strength is best demonstrated in restraint and in quiet confidence.
- We believe that we must become worldly wise and street-smart to make it in life. God tell us that we must become as children with a pure and simple faith.
- We believe pride in our achievements makes us pillars of success. The Word admonishes us to be humble, willing to associate with people of low position.
- We live to acquire and, if necessary, to keep others from doing so. Jesus taught us to give it all away, and store up treasures in heaven.
- We worry and stress; so many are consumed with psychosomatic symptoms. God tells us to be anxious about *nothing* and to trust and obey.

- So many of us serve God by doing as much as humanly possible, constantly. God desires that we abide with him and receive his peace that passes understanding.
- When we are hurt, we strike back, or wish we did. God tells us to bless those who persecute us.

We *all* see things through our own eyes and experience. God knows everything—no exaggeration, *everything*. Since this world is infected with sin, much of what is communicated through public channels is influenced by the father of lies. We *must* listen to that still small voice.

ONLY JESUS

Universalism is thought by some to be the rational and logical philosophy of reasonable people. How could *anyone* believe that *their* truth is absolute—that others' beliefs are not valid? People then dig into their positions and intransigence turns into vitriolic accusations and flying "isms." Political universalism questions the relationship between subjectivity and power, with a specific focus on human rights. Moral universalism believes that some system of ethics applies universally for all similarly situated individuals. Theological universalism believes that all human beings will find God in their own time and manner. It makes perfect sense, doesn't it?

You will need to decide for yourself. But first, ponder this statement: *Jesus is the only way to God.* From what authority is such a statement made?

- I am the way and the truth and the life. No one comes to the Father except through me. (John 14:6)

- Salvation is found in one else, for there is no other name under heaven given to mankind by which we must be saved. (Acts 4:12)
- Christ is the culmination of the law [of Moses] so that there may be righteousness for everyone who believes. (Rom. 10:4)
- I and the Father are one. (John 10:30)
- For in Christ all the fullness of the Deity lives in bodily form. (Col. 2:9)
- Now this is eternal life: that they know you, the only true God, and Jesus Christ, whom you have sent. (John 17:3)
- For even if there are so-called gods, whether in heaven or on earth (as indeed there are many "gods" and many "lords"), yet for us there is but one God, the Father, from whom all things came and for whom we live; and there is but one Lord, Jesus Christ, through whom all things came and through whom we live. (1 Cor. 8:5–6)

There are some marvelous things happening through the power of the Holy Spirit in our world today. More Muslims are coming to faith in Jesus Christ than any time in history. Jesus himself is appearing to thousands, perhaps millions, in dreams and visions to people all over the Middle East. This is occurring in Saudi Arabia, Iran, and all other Islamic countries caught between these Sunni and Shia polarities. I commend to you the book *Dreams and Visions*, by Tom Doyle; there are other informative books on this topic. Today in America the politically correct position believes it is abject foolishness to even suggest that Islam is not an equally legitimate path to God. However, if your authority is based on the Bible the answer is . . . only Jesus.

TRUSTFUL SURRENDER

Tom Sullivan is my special friend who gave me two books that blessed my journey of growth and discovery, for which I am eternally thankful. One of them was written in the seventeenth century by two Jesuits from France. The title is *Trustful Surrender to Divine Providence: The Secret of Peace and Happiness.*[2] There are also plenty of Scripture verses and hymns on this important topic; it seems a few people besides me had to wrestle with this life-changing decision. That's what it ultimately comes down to: *my* decision. *Your* decision.

Who else walked this path? Abraham and Sarah laughed at God over his promise that she would bear a child at her age. It took twenty-five years to come to pass, but it happened. Their sarcastic disbelief turned into trustful surrender. Jonah wasn't about to go to Nineveh when the Lord asked him to. It took a storm, falling overboard, and taking a deep dive inside a large sea creature to bring him to his senses. His willful disobedience turned into trustful surrender. Jeremiah was asked by God to specifically warn the people of Judah that they would suffer famine, foreign conquest, plunder, and captivity. He reluctantly complied and was beaten, put in stocks, and ridiculed in public as people passed. His discomfort and shame turned into trustful surrender. Job was near the top of God's list of the most faithful and righteous dudes in the land. But when Satan was given a limited opportunity to take a few whacks at him, even Job complained bitterly and wished he had never been born. He came to his senses and yielded to God in trustful surrender.

I have five single-spaced typed pages of notes and highlights from *Trustful Surrender.* From those, I'm inspired to share the following:

- Prosperity has the effect of softening us. Adversity, on the other hand, leads us naturally to raise our eyes to heaven to seek consolation in our distress.
- There is no tribulation or temptation where God has not appointed limits, so as to serve not for our destruction but for our salvation.
- Apart from sin, *nothing* happens to us in life unless God wills it so.
- It is foolish to think we can see better than God, who is not subject to the passions that blind us, knows the future, and can foresee all events and consequences.
- If I paid heed to what you think you need you would have been hopelessly ruined long ago. (God)
- All is vanity and nothing can satisfy my heart. The things that I so earnestly desire may not be at all the things that will bring me happiness.
- Whether the sea is calm or rough, whichever way the waves are carried by the wind, is a matter of indifference to him, for the place where he is, is firm and unshakable.

Let us then trust ourselves entirely to God and His Providence and leave Him complete power to order our lives, turning to Him lovingly in every need and awaiting His help without anxiety. Leave everything to Him and He will provide us with everything, at the time and in the place and in the manner best suited. He will lead us on our way to that happiness and peace of mind for which we are destined in this life as a foretaste of the everlasting happiness we have been promised.[3]

HEARING GOD

I exercise humility every leap year, have a healthy IQ, acerbic wit, supreme confidence, and relentless energy—OK, maybe four out of five! It isn't hard to imagine, then, how long it has taken me to *really* hear the voice of God. Except for my period of wandering, I kept a fairly consistent regimen of reading God's Word and other Christian literature, attending church and home groups, engaging in special times of quiet reflection, and more. Additionally, I was *doing* what I felt God wanted me to *do*, serving in a global ministry of mercy and compassion. But often my prayer time was rote and routine, mostly me talking and God listening . . . or was he? Since God already knows what we are going to ask, I suspect there were times when he pushed the mute button on my transmissions, because he had quite a lot of other things to attend to.

My Christian brother Phil Jemmett introduced me to his accountability partners, Johann De Villiers and Rand Mulford. I've heard them "give him a go" a number of times. When I was AWOL, there *was* no accountability partner. Rand gave me a two-CD teaching titled, "Hearing God's Voice."[4] This spiritual food brought both clarity and my renewed commitment to diligently seek God's voice.

In the original Greek language of the New Testament there are two distinct words translated as "word"—*logos* (λόγος) and *rhema* (ρήμα). Each have valuable meaning and purpose in our walk with God. In brief, *logos* is the written, recorded Word which represents the full mind and counsel of God. It is eternal, complete, settled. In the Gospel of John, we understand that Jesus became the incarnate Word (*logos*) to us in the flesh.

The second expression of the word, *rhema*, was the missing link in my experience. *Rhema* is God's spoken word measured out to us personally and presently. It imparts life, peace, and his divine presence. *Rhema* quickens the logos for our understanding and faith. "Man does not live by bread alone, but on every word [*rhema*] that comes from the mouth of God" (Matt. 4:4). "My sheep listen to my voice; I know them, and they follow me" (John 10:27). These are tangible blessings that are given to us when we hear God through his *rhema*—the spoken, quickened, living word:

- words of encouragement, for us and to give to others
- personal direction for each day
- a greater capacity to obey
- receiving strength for all our tasks and trials
- inspired determination to stay the course
- increased faith
- living an extraordinary life

Do you hear God's voice? I am not suggesting audibly, but whispered in quiet stillness, which comes after a time of intentional worship and communion with him, waiting on his presence. I had perfected the practice of reading black words on white pages. There was some value to this. But until I discovered and practiced active listening to God, my walk with him was self-directed and not intimate. Thankfully, that is changing.

ALWAYS PRAY

There are *so* many wonderful prayers in the Bible and exemplary teachers of prayer, most importantly the Lord Jesus. I will put David in *my* second position—shepherd, armor bearer, giant slayer, prince, king, adulterer, forgiven penitent, psalmist, ancestor of Jesus. I choose to share only one passage on prayer: "Be joyful in hope, patient in affliction, faithful in prayer" (Rom. 12:12). This short scripture encapsulates profound truth for *me*. Affliction is book-ended, hemmed-in by joy and hope, faithfulness, and prayer. It's a four-to-one certainty God will prevail!

In the year 2020, with COVID-19 raging around the globe, economic distress, places of worship closed, unrest and chaos in many cities of the world, and heightened geopolitical tension everywhere, I committed myself to more intense and intentional prayer. I formed an intercessor group of some 125 persons, mostly from the US but with a dozen international participants. I had secured permission in advance from about seventy-five of them, and later added about fifty friends and associates without notifying them in advance. During a fifteen-volume series I wrote which ran from April to December, I asked these faithful people to pray for many things. Each volume contained a themed commentary, supplemented by a list of global and individual prayer requests, both intentionally kept to one page.

I believe that some were too busy to pray, and some possibly never even opened my email with the attachments. Yet, I am also absolutely certain many did pray, faithfully. Some let me know by email, text, phone, or in person.

"I know that only in earnest supplication, and calm trust that the results, does a man learn strength and gain peace. Therefore, I have laid incessant, persistent pleading as a duty upon my disciples. Prayer changes all. Prayer re-creates. Prayer is irresistible. So, pray literally, without ceasing, never weary in prayer. When one day man sees how marvelously his prayer has been answered, then he will deeply, so deeply, regret that he prayed so little."[5] As you read these standing prayer requests and feel motivated to pray, please remember these matters in your time with the Lord:

- That God's will and purpose is accomplished, that his kingdom will come on earth as it is in heaven.
- That the Holy Spirit will be poured out mightily on the United States and every country of the world to bring people to repentance, leading to revival.
- That Jesus's name will be known, glorified, and received in all lands where political and religious intolerance and persecution is harshly enforced.
- That all people in bondage—physical, emotional, and spiritual: addictions, sexual, human trafficking, compulsive behavior, and forced labor—are set free.
- That those parts of the global Christian church, believers, the bride of Christ—who are slumbering, hesitating, waiting, or unengaged—will *awaken* and understand that the time is *now* to pray and fight. Each one of us is just one last heartbeat from eternity.
- For God's healing touch on ailing bodies—for all illness, surgeries, hospitalizations, and calamities, until we are given our new heavenly body.
- For healing in all broken or estranged relationships—in families, communities, and nations, where love conquers all.

LOVE CONQUERS

The most significant discovery God allowed me *now* to fully comprehend is that love is intended to be both the journey and the destination. "God must be our first love because only then can he teach us . . . All other things we put first in our lives make bad gods that will let us down . . . Love is, without a doubt, the basis for everything. Each and every one of us is deeply known and cared for by a Creator who cherishes us beyond any ability we have to comprehend. That knowledge must no longer remain a secret."[6] Through the days of my youth, the years of preparation, decades of service, a period of wandering, and events of both significance and trial, God's love allowed me to conquer, to prosper, and to take hold of the victory he won on the cross. These are just a few incarnational examples that I discovered on *my* journey:

- Love conquered my fear (I John 4:18).
- Love was a light on every turn and stretch of my path (Ps. 119:105).
- Love is still teaching me to love my neighbor as myself (Mark 12:33).
- Love is still refining me to be patience and release wrongs (1 Cor. 13:4–5).
- Love reminded me that *everything* good comes from God—all of creation, love, light, goodness, color, music, the laughter of children, family, and especially friendship. (*Thank you, Bill Barta, for your enduring support and faithful prayers in friendship over so many years!*)
- Love punctuated the truth that oneness with God is the goal of my existence.

- Love conquers hate, evil, injustice, and oppression, and will until the end, when God wins and we are welcomed into eternity.

"Only what is done in Love lasts, for God is love, and only the work of God remains. The test of all true work and words is—are they inspired by Love? If man only saw how vain is so much of his activity! SO much work done in my name is not acknowledged by Me. As for love: turn out from your hearts and lives all that is not loving, so shall you bear much fruit, and by this all men shall know you are my disciples, because you have Love one toward another."[7]

GOD WINS

From the moment of the fall of man—depicted in Genesis 3 all the way through John 3, when God revealed how much he loved the world—the final victory has never been in doubt. We cannot fully comprehend, on this side of eternity, *why* God chose to structure salvation history in the manner he did. God is love. Jesus is the way. After all our asking, analyzing, doubting, grumbling, wandering, we have *the choice*, the free will, to not be in the presence of our Creator for eternity—*or*, we can trust and obey. There is no other way.

My life has indeed been a bold and dashing adventure. Had I fully understood these profound eternal truths and followed them sooner I would have been much wiser. I'm not singing Sinatra's "I Did it My Way." Instead I am awed, humbled by God's amazing grace, unfathomable mercy, long suffering and unending love. This is beautifully depicted in the worship song "Resurrecting" by Elevation Worship.[8] Seven stanzas will be our benediction!

*The head that once was crowned with thorns is crowned
with glory now*
The Savior knelt to wash our feet, now at his feet we bow
The One who wore our sin and shame now robed in majesty
The radiance of perfect love now shines for all to see
*The fear that held us now gives way to Him who is our
peace*
His final breath upon the cross is now alive in me
*The tomb where soldiers watched in vain was borrowed for
three days*
*His body there would not remain, our God has robbed the
grave*
Your name, your name is victory
All praise, will rise to Christ our King
By your spirit I will rise from the ashes of defeat
The resurrected King is resurrecting me
In your name I come alive to declare your victory
The resurrected King is resurrecting me.

AMEN

Recommended Reading

The following ten books have played a significant role in my spiritual journey. Therefore, I recommend them to you as well. They each address some element of life challenge, searching, growing in Christ, wandering or being found! Blessings to you.

Baker, Mark W. *Overcoming Shame: Let Go of Others' Expectations and Embrace God's Acceptance.* Eugene, OR: Harvest House, 2018.

Craft, Charles H. *The Evangelical's Guide to Spiritual Warfare: Scriptural Insights and Practical Instruction on Facing the Enemy.* Bloomington, MN: Chosen Books, 2015.

Eldredge, John. *Moving Mountains: Praying with Passion, Confidence and Authority.* Nashville: Thomas Nelson, 2016.

Godwin, Roy, and Dave Roberts. *The Grace Outpouring: Becoming a People of Blessing.* Colorado Springs: David C. Cook, 2012.

Nouwen, Henri J. M. *The Return of the Prodigal Son: A Story of Homecoming.* New York: Image Books, 1994.

Orr, J. Edwin. *Full Surrender.* London: Marshall, Morgan & Scott, Ltd., 1957.

Przybylski, Debbie. *Intercessors Arise: Personal Prayer That Changes the World.* Charleston, SC: CreateSpace, 2014.

Russell, A.J., ed. *God Calling: A Devotional Diary.* Alresford, UK: Circle Books, 2017.

Saint-Jure, Jean Baptiste and Claude de la Colombière. *Trustful Surrender to Divine Providence: The Secret of Peace and Happiness.* Charlotte, NC: TAN Books, 2012.

Young, William Paul. *The Shack: Where Tragedy Confronts Eternity.* Newbury Park, CA: Windblown Media, 2007.

Contact the Author

*A*s Dr. Mark Baker so accurately stated in his Foreword, "Men were not raised to be vulnerable and honest about their emotions, especially with other men . . . Today, especially, men need to admit when we get lost, ask for help, and open up about how we feel."

While I am not a licensed psychologist, I was an ordained minister and Navy chaplain. But more importantly, I have traveled much on the road of life, and *may* have encountered some of what you are going through.

If you want to be in contact, please feel free to write to me. Two options are below.

Peace to you, on your journey.

Ralph Edward Plumb
www.drralphplumb.com
ralpheplumb@gmail.com

Endnotes

Preface

1   Gregory David Roberts, *Shantaram* (London: Time Warner, 2004), 933.

Introduction

1   I served eight years in the Individual Ready Reserve (IRR) with active duty mostly with the 1st Marines—Camp Pendleton, Marine Amphibious Force (MAF); also, Marine Air Wing (MAW), and Marine Mountain Warfare Training Center.

Chapter 1: On the Road

1   Established by Chinese Leader Deng Xioping in 1979, the One Child Policy was concerned with curtailing the rapid growth of the population, then at about one billion. It required that all majority Han Chinese families could only birth one child. The law was revoked by Xi Jinping in 2016.

2   The Three-Self Patriotic Movement, colloquially called the Three Self Church, was established in 1954 and administered by the State Administration for Religious Affairs. Its expressed goal is to control the growth and message of Christianity.

3   A. J. Russell, ed. *God Calling* (Uhrichsville, OH: Barbour Publishers, 1998), December 9.

Chapter 2: Time and Eternity

1   Daniela Hernandez and Brianna Abbott, "Scientists Release First Image of a Black Hole," *The Wall Street Journal*, April 10, 2019,

https://www.wsj.com/articles/scientists-release-first-image-of-a-black-hole-11554908995.

2   "What Were Stephen Hawking's Last Words?" Quora, https://www.quora.com/What-were-Stephen-Hawkings-last-words#:~:text=Stephen%20Hawking's%20last%20words%20were,of%20the%20preciousness%20of%20time%E2%80%9D.&text=He%20said%2C%E2%80%9D%20There's%20nothing%20like%20heaven%20or%20hell.%E2%80%9D.

3   Sam Jones, "Steve Jobs's Last Words: 'Oh wow. Oh wow. Oh wow,'" *The Guardian*, Oct. 31, 2011, https://www.theguardian.com/technology/2011/oct/31/steve-jobs-last-words.

4   The Youngbloods, "Get Together," by Chet Powers, recorded 1966, track 4 on *The Youngbloods*, RCA Victor, 1967, vinyl LP.

5   The "Fertile Crescent" was a term coined by American archeologist James Henry in 1914 to describe the region of the Middle East fed by the Euphrates, Tigris, and Nile rivers creating the rich soils to grow abundant crops. Also called the Cradle of Civilization—comprised of land now partially included in the sovereign nations of Egypt, Jordan, Lebanon, Israel, Syria, Turkey, Iran, Iraq, and Cyprus—it is considered the birthplace of humankind.

6   Yahweh or Jehovah was originally referred to as YHWH (ה ו ה י), also referred to by scholars as the tetragrammaton.

7   You can learn more about Manara Ministries at www.brighthopeworld.com.

8   Agnes Sanford, *The Healing Light* (New York: Ballantine Books, 1972). Excerpt taken from Jonathan Hunter, *Embracing Life Series* (Maitland, FL: Xulon Press, 1998), 103.

Chapter 3: Doing or Being

1   Gary L. Nederveld Associates Grand Haven, MI (seven hundred employees, most registered physical therapists).

2   "St. Teresa of Calcutta," Catholic Online, https://www.catholic.org/saints/saint.php?saint_id=5611.

3   Marc Fey, Don Ankenbrandt, and Frank Johnson, *210 Project: Discover Your Place in God's Story* (Birmingham, AL: Alliance Publ. Group, 2011), 44.

4   Russell, *God Calling*, September 15.

5   Robert D. Kaplan, *Balkan Ghosts: A Journey through History* (New York: Vintage Books, 1994), 22.

6   *The Hiding Place*, directed by James F. Collier (1975), motion picture.

7   Gerard Kelly and Lowell Shepherd, *Miracle in Mostar* (Oxford: Lion Books, 1995), 28.

Chapter 4: Wisdom or Knowledge

1   The San peoples, also known as Bushmen, are an indigenous hunter-gatherer people and the original inhabitants of southern Africa.

2   Elizabeth J. Jewell, ed, *The Oxford Desk Dictionary & Thesaurus* (Oxford: Oxford University Press, 2002), 459.

3   The Scientific Method has been used since ancient times, but was first documented by Sir Francis Bacon in the early 1600s.

4   www.vrbo.com April 2019 National Ad Campaign. Produced by Prettybird. Directed by Todd Strauss-Schulson.

Chapter 5: Fatherhood

1   The use of masculine third-person personal pronouns such as he/him/his when referring to the three persons of the Godhead follow the historic norms of our global cultures and does not refer to sex or gender. This does not comport with twenty-first-century revisionist thinking on gender or the use of pronouns.

2   "The Proof Is In: Father Absence Harms Children," National Fatherhood Initiative, https://www.fatherhood.org/father-absence-statistic.

3   Barack Obama, "Obama's Father's Day Remarks," *The New York Times*, June 15, 2008, https://www.nytimes.com/2008/06/15/us/politics/15text-obama.html.

4   "A Tree Grows in Selma—The Alton Hardy Story," Epic Classroom and Culture, https://classroomandculture.libsyn.com/size/5/?search=alton+hardy.

Chapter 6: Being a Father

1   Ralph Plumb, "Ralph's Story," YouTube video, 6:05, April 3, 2013, http://youtu.be/H2_FxW7bLjw.

2   John Eldredge, *Moving Mountains: Praying with Passion, Confidence, and Authority* (Nashville: Nelson Books, 2016), 158.

Chapter 7: Freedom Is Not Free

1   Westminster Confession of Faith, https://www.ligonier.org/learn/articles/westminster-confession-faith.

2   Oliver L. North, *One More Mission: Oliver North Returns to Vietnam* (Grand Rapids: Zondervan; New York: HarperCollins, 1993), 214.

Chapter 8: The Frog in the Kettle

1   For more information on Lorma Medical Center and Lorma Schools see www.lorma.org.

2   "Trafficking Terms," Shared Hope International, https://sharedhope.org/the-problem/trafficking-terms.

3   "Addictions," HealthyPlace, https://www.healthyplace.com/addictions.

4   *Oxford Desk Dictionary & Thesaurus*, 84.

5   Charles H. Craft, *The Evangelical's Guide to Spiritual Warfare: Scriptural Insights and Practical Instruction on Facing the Enemy* (Bloomington, MN: Chosen Books, 2015), 30.

6   Henri J. M. Nouwen, *The Return of the Prodigal Son: A Story of Homecoming* (New York: Image Books, 1994), 82.

Chapter 9: The Enemy Is the Enemy

1   Hannah Ritchie, Joe Hasell, Cameron Appel, and Max Roser, "Terrorism," Our World in Data, last updated November 2019, https://ourworldindata.org/terrorism.

2   "Technicals" or NSTVs—non-standard technical vehicles—played an important role in the 1990s Somali Civil War and the 2006–2009 War in Somalia. They were four-wheel-drive pickup trucks with machine gun, anti-aircraft gun, rotary cannon, anti-tank weapon, mortar, rocket launcher, or some other mounted weapon.

3   UNOSOM—United Nations Assistance Mission in Somalia—was a multilateral force comprised of 22,000 troops and 8,000 logistics and civilian staff; https://unsom.unmissions.org.

4   The Green Zone, also called Halane, was the heavily guarded international quadrant with mostly African Union Mission Troops to keep government and nongovernmental organizations safe.

5   Craft, *Evangelical's Guide to Spiritual Warfare*, back cover.

6   Ibid., 24.

7   John Piper, "Satan's Ten Strategies Against You," DesiringGod, October 4, 2016, https://www.desiringgod.org/articles/satans-ten-strategies-against-you.Ibid.

8   Craft, *Evangelical's Guide to Spiritual Warfare*, 17.

9   Eldredge, *Moving Mountains*, 200.

10   Paula White Cain, *Something Greater: Finding Triumph over Trials* (New York: Hachette, 2019), 167.

Chapter 10: Wandering

1   Dr. Ralph E. Plumb and Dr. Feager A. Pertilla, *My Mother Your Mama: Stories about Caring for Aging Parents* (Bloomington. IN: Westbow Press. 2017).

2   J. Edwin Orr, *Full Surrender,* reprint (Goleta, CA: Enduring Word. 2017), 15.

3   Nouwen, *Return of the Prodigal Son*, 44.

Chapter 11: Hidden or Transparent

1   Orr, *Full Surrender*, 46–47.

2   United Nations Development Programme (UNDP), www.undp.org.

3   John Lennon, "Imagine," recorded May 1971, track 1 on *Imagine*, Apple, vinyl LP.

4   Joseph M. Stowell, et al., *The CoMission: The Amazing Story of Eighty Ministry Groups Working Together to Take the Message of Christ's Love to the Russian People* (Chicago: Moody Press. 2004).

5   Mark W. Baker, *Overcoming Shame: Let Go of Others' Expectations and Embrace God's Acceptance* (Eugene: OR: Harvest House, 2018), 23.

Chapter 12: Grace and Mercy

1   Katherine Spinky, *Mother Teresa: A Complete Authorized Biography* (New York: Harper Collins, 1997), 55.

2   The Evangelical Alliance Mission (TEAM), www.team.org.

3   Monkey Temple or Swayambhu—meaning "self-existent one," a thirteenth-century Buddhist shrine.

4   Ron Hall and Denver Moore, *Same Kind of Different as Me* (Nashville: W Publishing Group, 2006), back cover.

5   You can find out more about Beverly McNeil's gallery at www.portraitsinc.com.

6   More information about the Lovelady Center is available at www.loveladycenter.org.

Chapter 13: Forgiveness and Healing

1   Jeff Reinke, *Men's Skills*, North Coast Calvary Chapel, Carlsbad, CA, 2011.

2   Henri J. M. Nouwen, *The Wounded Healer* (New York: Convergent Books, 2017).

3   Reinke, *Men's Skills*, chapter 10, page 2.

4   Eldredge, *Moving Mountains,* 195.

5   Reinke, *Men's Skills*, chapter 10, page 8.

6   Leo Buscaglia, https://quotefancy.com/quote/758224/Leo-Buscaglia-
     Love-yourself-accept-yourself-forgive-yourself-and-be-good-to-yourself.

7   More information about AMEXTRA is available at www.amextra.org.

8   William Arthur Ward, https://quotefancy.com/quote/933977/
     William-Arthur-Ward-We-are-most-like-beasts-when-we-kill-We-are-
     most-like-men-when-we.

Chapter 14: What Really Matters

1   James Aughey was a minister imprisoned and condemned to execution
     for his outspoken anti-succession and pro-Union beliefs. He escaped.

2   Fr. Jean Baptiste, St. Claude de la Colombier. *Trustful Surrender to
     Divine Providence: The Secret of Peace and Happiness* (Gastonia, NC:
     TAN Books, 2012).

3   Ibid., 128–29.

4   Derek Prince, "Hearing God's Voice," 2 CDs, https://www.
     derekprince.org/shop/sections/items/item.aspx?item_id=1000035091.

5   Russell, *God Calling*, May 16.

6   John Burke, *Imagine Heaven: Near-Death Experiences: God's Promises,
     and the Exhilarating Future That Awaits You* (Grand Rapids, MI: Baker
     Books. 2015), 148.

7   Russell, *God Calling*, November 22.

8   Elevation Worship, "Resurrecting," by Chris Brown, Mack Brock,
     Matthews Ntlele, Steven Furtick, and Wade Joye, recorded July 31,
     2015, track 5 on *Here as in Heaven*. Essential Worship/Provident Label
     Group, 2016, CD.

CPSIA information can be obtained
at www.ICGtesting.com
Printed in the USA
JSHW052034111222
34732JS00006B/50